Rita Levi-Montalcini

Nobel Prize Winner

Women in Medicine

Rita Levi-Montalcini

Nobel Prize Winner

Susan Tyler Hitchcock

CHELSEA HOUSE
PUBLISHERS
A Haights Cross Communications Company
Philadelphia

COVER: Rita Levi-Montalcini, in her laboratory at Washington University, in St. Louis, 1963. Rita left Italy for St. Louis in 1946 at the invitation of Viktor Hamburger, for what she thought would be a six- to nine-month research assignment. Rita, however, remained in the United States for many years, doing research that led to the discovery of nerve growth factor (NGF), which eventually earned her a Nobel Prize.

CHELSEA HOUSE PUBLISHERS
VP, NEW PRODUCT DEVELOPMENT Sally Cheney
DIRECTOR OF PRODUCTION Kim Shinners
CREATIVE MANAGER Takeshi Takahashi
MANUFACTURING MANAGER Diann Grasse

Staff for RITA LEVI-MONTALCINI
EXECUTIVE EDITOR Lee M. Marcott
PHOTO EDITOR Sarah Bloom
PRODUCTION EDITOR Noelle Nardone
SERIES & COVER DESIGNER Takeshi Takahashi
LAYOUT 21st Century Publishing and Communications, Inc.

A Haights Cross Communications ✈ Company

http://www.chelseahouse.com

First Printing

9 8 7 6 5 4 3 2 1

Library of Congress Cataloging-in-Publication Data

Hitchcock, Susan Tyler.
    Rita Levi-Montalcini / Susan Tyler Hitchcock.
      p. cm.—(Women in medicine)
    ISBN 0-7910-8028-5
    1. Levi-Montalcini, Rita. 2. Neurologists—Biography. 3. Developmental neurobiology. 4. Nerve growth factor. 5. Nobel Prizes. I. Title. II. Series.
RC339.52.L48H54 2004
616.8'092—dc22

                                                          2004006050

All links and web addresses were checked and verified to be correct at the time of publication. Because of the dynamic nature of the web, some addresses and links may have changed since publication and may no longer be valid.

Table of Contents

Science in Hiding 1

Throughout all of Rita Levi-Montalcini's childhood, life for a Jewish girl in northern Italy had been difficult. In 1939, though, as she turned 30, life for her turned dangerous.

A young scientist with a medical degree from the University of Turin, Levi-Montalcini was attending a conference in Stockholm, Sweden, on September 1, 1939. The news came with a jolt: Germany had invaded Poland. Hitler and his Nazi regime were on a path to overtake all of Europe. With the Fascist Benito Mussolini as prime minister, Italy seemed destined to ally with Germany. Politics in Italy were mirroring those in Germany, and anti-Semitism, prejudice against Jewish people, was becoming the official way of life in Italian cities. In the past 18 months, events had shocked all those who believed in tolerance and compassion. The government actually was passing laws that forbid Jews to live a normal life in Italy. They could not marry non-Jews, teach in public schools, serve in the military, or even own a radio. Mussolini arranged for a manifesto to be signed by 10 so-called scientists—Levi-Montalcini recognized only two of the names—declaring that "the Jews did not belong to the Italian race." [1] By October 1938, all the Jewish scientists, professors, and intellectuals of Italy were barred from the country's universities. And now, with Hitler's invasion of Poland, anti-Semitism was aligning with war. The national policy of hatred for the Jews could turn violent.

For months, Rita Levi-Montalcini and members of her family had been living in Belgium, trying to escape the terrors mounting in Turin, their home city in the north of Italy. But now, with Germany on the offensive, even Belgium felt unsafe to them. When, on Christmas Eve 1939, Mussolini publicly declared that his country would not go to war, Italy seemed a safer haven, and many Italian Jews, including the Levi-Montalcinis, returned home. Their hopes were dashed, though, five months later, when Italy formed an alliance, called the Pact of Steel, with Germany, and the two countries became military allies against the Allied forces of France, Britain, and, later, the United States.

NIPPED IN THE BUD

For Rita Levi-Montalcini, it could not have been a worse time to be forced to leave the university laboratory and the scientific work she had been conducting. She had graduated from medical school in 1936, passionately interested in continuing her studies on the growth of nerve cells and nervous systems. Working under the great anatomist Giuseppe Levi, who was also a Jew forced to flee the Fascists, Levi-Montalcini had learned the delicate techniques of preparing living tissue to view under the microscope. Using a scalpel to make slices of tissue just one cell thick, she had begun her studies by laboriously counting cells under the microscope. Now, a scientist on her own, she had become interested in the patterns through which cells migrated as they developed from a tiny, newly conceived bundle of undifferentiated cells into a complex nervous system, with cells assigned to perform different functions. She used chicken eggs to conduct her studies, methodically viewing, over and over again, the cell structure of the growing spinal column in chick embryos from 1 to 20 days old, just before the chick hatches. She carefully tapped into eggshells and attached electrodes to tiny spots in the live embryos, then observed the signals transmitted through those electrodes on the screen of an oscilloscope, a device that graphs changes in electrical charge over time. At other times she removed bits of tissue from inside the egg and injected a chemical solution of silver into the specimen, highlighting certain features more clearly for view under the microscope. She made drawings of what she found, building a frame-by-frame progression of nerve cell growth during the chicken embryo's first weeks of life.

But now war and prejudice put an end to those studies. For a while, anxious to do something worthwhile, Rita Levi-Montalcini practiced medicine. She visited other Jews in hiding, the elderly or sick who needed medical attention, but did not dare to visit a non-Jewish doctor's office. She was breaking the law by practicing her profession but, as Levi-Montalcini wrote years later, "These poor people, who lived in the attics of houses in old Turin, did not care about the laws and were glad of my visits and the help I could offer within the limits of my scarce finances." [2] The trouble was, only Aryan (non-Jewish) physicians could write legal prescriptions for medicine, so Levi-Montalcini could only diagnose and advise.

In these anxious times, friends meant so much. One day she had a visit from Rodolpho Amprino. They had met in medical school. Amprino, like most Italian citizens, did not agree with the anti-Semitic laws in his country, but he had to visit Levi-Montalcini in secret, for both his and her sake. When he heard that she had abandoned her laboratory experiments, he encouraged her to do otherwise.

"One doesn't lose heart in the face of the first difficulties," he advised her. He reminded her of the great Spanish neuro-scientist, Santiago Ramón y Cajal, born in 1852 and winner of the 1906 Nobel Prize in Medicine. "Remember Ramón y Cajal who, in a poorly equipped institute, in the sleepy city that Valencia must have been in the middle of the last century, did the fundamental work that established the basis of all we know about the nervous system of vertebrates," Amprino told her with conviction. "Set up a small laboratory and take up your interrupted research." [3]

A CLANDESTINE LABORATORY

Inspired, Rita Levi-Montalcini turned her little bedroom into a science laboratory. It was easy to get chicken eggs because everyone assumed she was feeding her family. It was not as easy to find the instruments she needed, but she made a list of essentials: an incubator, the silver stain, a microtome (an instrument that cuts thin slices of tissue for microscopic examination), two microscopes including one with a camera, and a few common surgical instruments. She somehow collected all these without arousing attention. She got forceps from a watchmaker and tiny scissors from a friendly oph- thalmologist. She used a fine-grained grindstone to sharpen common sewing needles into tiny scalpels. Her brother built her a glass case, into which she could slip her hands and operate on the embryos, and through which she could view her work in the microscope. If curious friends asked what she was doing, her mother told them she was operating and could not be disturbed. [4]

All through the winter and spring of 1941, in her makeshift bedroom laboratory, Rita Levi-Montalcini contin- ued the work that she loved the best: observing and recording the patterns of nerve growth in developing embryos. She con- sidered how cells in the developing nervous system influenced those in other systems, primarily muscle cells and sensory cells. Outside, on the streets, Fascist posters threatened to torture and kill all Jews, but inside her tiny room, Rita Levi-Montalcini persisted.

She read constantly, informing her own work with the find- ings of others, essential to the progress of any scientist. Nearly 50 years later, as she wrote her autobiography, Levi-Montalcini remembered a key moment in her thinking—so important, in fact, she called it a "conversion."

> After war had been declared, civilian trains were taken over for troop transportation, and these livestock trains, or cattle cars, were used for civilians, for short journeys in the provinces. The wagons, which lacked seats, doors, and windows, offered great panoramic views through the windowless open sides . . . I sat down in what was considered to be one of the best places—the floor of the wagon—with my legs dangling over the side in the open air. . . . While enjoying the view and the air which smelled of hay, I was distractedly reading an article [Giuseppe] Levi had given to me two years before. [5]

The article was written by embryologist Viktor Hamburger, a German embryologist working at Washington University in St. Louis, Missouri. In his work, Hamburger had removed the budding wings of chick embryos, then observed how that operation affected the development of the central nervous system. A week after he removed the limb bud, Hamburger reported, the portion of the spinal cord that would have served that wing was much smaller than normal. Without the cells destined to become the wing itself, in other words, muscle and nerve cells destined to operate that wing did not develop normally. How did it happen that events in the damaged wing area influenced the growing pattern of cells some distance away, in the spinal column?

VIKTOR HAMBURGER'S INDUCTIVE FACTOR

Hamburger's hypothesis was that cells in the "peripheral field," that is, cells in the outer part of the developing body, "do take part in the growth control of their own centers," or the nerve and muscle systems that will control them. [6] In a normally growing wing, something communicated to the earliest nerve cells developing in the spinal column, prompting nerve growth in the pattern needed later for sensation and motion. If the wing was absent, no such signal reached the cells in the spinal column.

Lights went on in Rita Levi-Montalcini's head as she read these ideas, which connected so intimately with the observations she had been making in her bedroom laboratory. Later, she would look back at that 1934 article by Viktor Hamburger and call it her "Bible." [7] "I don't know how far the idyllic circumstances in which I read the article contributed to my desire to delve into this phenomenon," she wrote in her autobiography, "but in memory my decision is indissolubly bound up with that summer afternoon and the smell of hay wafting into the wagon. I did not imagine at the time, however, that this interest and my subsequent research would determine my future." [8]

Levi-Montalcini returned to her hidden lab, energized by new questions, and spent the first months of 1942 probing them. Using the silver stain procedure, she found that nerve cells do continue to grow toward a limb bud that has been removed, but that once those growing cells reach the stump of the amputated limb, they begin to die, as if they were not receiving the nourishment they needed. "Their death appeared to be caused by the absence of a trophic factor"—a factor relating to nutrition—rather than Hamburger's "inductive one"—a trigger to start up nerve growth. [9]

It was a small distinction, one of interest only to those deeply involved in the study of cell growth. Years later, Levi-Montalcini reflected in her autobiography,

> I often asked myself how we could have dedicated ourselves with such enthusiasm to solving this small neuroembryological problem while German armies were advancing throughout Europe, spreading destruction and death wherever they went and threatening the very survival of Western civilization. The answer lies in the desperate and partially unconscious desire of human beings to ignore what is happening in situations where full awareness might lead one to self-destruction. [10]

NERVE CELLS UNDER THE MICROSCOPE

During the second half of 1942, war raged in the skies over Italy. German and Italian planes bombed Malta, a British island south of Sicily. In October, the British Royal Air Force began retaliating, bombing the cities of Genoa and Turin. Residents of Turin, including Rita Levi-Montalcini and her family, fled north into the highlands at the foot of the

Italian Alps. An hour from Turin, they could see their city's
night sky lit up by bomb flares and burning buildings. As
distressing as that was to someone who loved the city she
grew up in, the dedicated young scientist still did not give
up her pursuits. She had carried her primitive equipment
with her and set up a country laboratory. During the day,
Levi-Montalcini made the rounds of farms nearby, begging
farmers to sell her fertilized chicken eggs. Food was so scarce
that after she removed cells from eggs, she cooked them for
family suppers. When her brother discovered that, he
refused to eat her omelets.

Often, Levi-Montalcini traveled into Turin. Nights
there were filled with devastation, but days were eerily
serene. "The ruins of bombed buildings, broken pipelines,
damaged electrical and telephone plants were swept aside
and repaired with unbelievable speed," she later wrote,
"but hopelessness and despair were written on everybody's
face." [11] Amid these conditions, Levi-Montalcini kept
her university professor, Giuseppe Levi, apprised of her
progress. She was moving forward in experiments that
forged the path that she would follow for many years to
come. The central theme of her investigations, in her own
words, was "the study of the interaction of genetic and
environmental factors in the regulation of the differentiation processes of the nervous system during the early
stages of its development." [12] What had once been the stuff
of textbooks and complicated journal articles was now
becoming her own, she recognized one day as she gazed
out her window at the countryside of northern Italy.
She watched a mother duck, followed by her ducklings,
waddling in a single-file line down the road, diving now
and then into puddles formed by rain in the ditches. In a
moment of revelation, she realized that the cells she had
been observing acted much like those ducklings, moving
together and following in a line.

> In specific areas of the embryonic nervous system, cells in the first stages of differentiation detach themselves from cellular clusters . . . and move singularly, one after the other like the little ducklings, toward distant locations along rigidly programmed routes, as is demonstrated by the fact that . . . these migrations are identical [in space and time] in different embryos. [13]

"Might I be seeing these things differently because I am here in the country, watching the natural world as it grows and moves in its many directions?" Levi-Montalcini asked herself.

> The fact that I was for the first time observing natural phenomena unknown to those who live in the cities, such as the springtime awakening of nature, cheered me and stimulated my interest in studying the developing nervous system. Now the nervous system appeared to me in a different light from its description in textbooks of neuroanatomy, where its structure is described as rigid and unchangeable. Only by following from hour to hour in different specimens, as in a cinematographic sequence, the development of nerve centers and circuits, did I come to realize how dynamic these processes are; how individual cells behave in a way similar to that of living beings; how plastic and malleable is the entire nervous system. [14]

Despite the hardships that persecution and war had forced upon her, Rita Levi-Montalcini had persisted in her science. She found comfort and satisfaction in the life of the mind. To so many of her fellow compatriots, those dark days were filled with nothing but terror, hatred, and destruction. To Rita Levi-Montalcini, when she looked back, they were the days in which she blossomed as a neuroscientist, making inroads essential to her future.

This system, which more than any other must adapt its structure and functions to environmental requirements, was to remain the main object of my research in the years that followed. Its analysis came into focus and grew in that country milieu probably much better than it would have in an academic institution. [15]

Focusing on work no matter what the circumstances, making progress despite obstacles all around her, Rita Levi-Montalcini strode forward, learning the lessons of science and the lessons of life that would elevate her to a position of world renown in the decades to come.

Growing Up in Turin

1909–1929

2

A NORTH ITALIAN GIRLHOOD

Rita Levi-Montalcini was one of four children growing up in a household in the north of Italy, the Piedmont, as it called, meaning the "foot of the mountains." From Turin, their home-town and capital of the Piedmont, they could see the Italian Alps. Less than a century before Levi-Montalcini's birth, the region had been a country on its own, called the Duchy of Savoy. Gardens and fountains, palaces and museums still recalled those ancient times in Turin, renowned as a center of art and politics since the Renaissance. Turin was also considered the birthplace of religious tolerance and nationalism in Italy. Jewish immigrants from France and Spain had been welcomed into Savoy for centuries, and they played important roles in Turin's intellectual and business community. When, in 1861, the many small nation–states on the Italian peninsula agreed to unite into a single nation, Turin was Italy's first capital city.

All of these lines of heritage made a difference in the Levi-Montalcini household. As a girl, Rita looked out the window of her family's fourth-floor apartment onto a grandiose statue of Vittorio Emanuele II, the king who succeeded in unifying Italy. "His gigantic figure which, unlike those of the other national heroes, rested on a pedestal taller than the surrounding nineteenth-century buildings, stood out against the gray winter sky with the majesty proper to a the king who, in 1870, brought about national unity," she wrote in her autobiography. For her, this regal figure always seemed to wear a "haughty, frowning gaze." She preferred his son, Umberto I, called "the good king" by the people of Turin. Both father and son sported massive, curving mustaches, as did many a man in Turin, including Rita's own father. She said she would rather kiss the air than kiss her father and get a bristly mustache in her face. [16]

In their youth, both of her parents had moved to the city of Turin from small towns nearby. Both were from Jewish families, but neither was devoutly observant. Her mother,

Adele, observed the Jewish traditions and holidays, though, while her father, Adamo, identified himself as a "freethinker," trusting more in his intellect than in religious faith. Sometimes their different approaches to religion caused friction in the household. On Passover, a Jewish holy day, Adamo Levi-Montalcini participated in the family ceremony, but he would interrupt solemn readings of scripture with sneers, snorts, and skeptical comments, infuriating his wife and her relatives but encouraging his children to think for themselves.

Of Rita Levi-Montalcini's three siblings, two were older. Her brother Gino and sister Anna were seven and five years older, respectively, than she was. The other sibling, her twin sister Paola, was her constant companion in childhood. Nonidentical twins, they did not look alike: Paola was three inches shorter and resembled their father, with a high forehead and deep-set blue eyes, while Rita's eyes were gray-green, like her mother's. Rita's passion was for the sciences, but Paola from her youngest years showed a talent for art. She matured into a painter and sculptor, inspired by Turin surrealist Giorgio de Chirico, and her art came to be well-known and well-regarded, especially in her home country. While Rita and Paola chose different life paths, their bond never weakened. Late in life, they would become constant companions once again, sharing an apartment in Rome. As an elderly woman, Rita came to recognize that despite their different paths in life, she and her sister had much in common. "There's no difference between us two, since my scientific bent and her artistic bent arise from the same intuitive faculty,"[17] wrote Rita.(For additional information on Rita's twin sister, enter "Paola Levi-Montalcini" into a search engine and browse the sites listed.)

GROWING UP IN THE MUSSOLINI ERA

All the Levi-Montalcini children inherited a fierce work ethic from their father. An engineer by training, Adamo

Levi-Montalcini was also an industrial visionary. His first project, after graduating from the Turin Polytechnic School, had been to build an ice factory and alcohol distillery in the town of Bari, a town on the east coast of southern Italy, overlooking the Adriatic Sea. In the first years of the twentieth century, ice was a rarity, and the butchers of Bari still kept meat cold with snow hauled down from the mountains in carts and stored in underground tunnels. Levi-Montalcini's ice-making establishment both amazed and threatened the people of Bari.

"Never before had they seen ice," wrote Levi-Montalcini, looking back on her father's life nearly 80 years later. "The owners of the stored snow, alarmed at the idea of losing their customers, spread the rumor that the young Jewish engineer who had landed on them from the north was an emissary of the devil." They called the ice glass and said it would "bore holes in Christian guts." [18] With passion for his work and a friendly attitude despite opposition, Adamo Levi-Montalcini won supporters in Bari and went on to build a distillery as well. During Rita and Paola's childhood, in the second decade of the twentieth century, he intended to build an ice factory and a distillery in Turin.

As Paola and Rita reached their teenage years, their father was facing a different threat to his business enterprises. More and more often, comments that he was Jewish carried ominous meaning, given the changing political climate in all of Italy. Rita Levi-Montalcini dates her awareness of these changes to June 11, 1924, when Giacomo Matteotti, a Socialist leader and member of Parliament who led a campaign against the Fascists, another political party, disappeared while walking to work in Rome one day. Two 10-year-olds reported that they had seen him grabbed off the street and thrown into a car. The license plate they reported belonged to a Fascist gang leader named Amerigo Dumini. A few weeks later, a decomposed body was found, and investigations confirmed that Matteotti had been murdered. Suspicions quickly surfaced that Benito Mussolini, prime minister of Italy since 1922, had ordered the assassination of this man whose politics did not match his own.

Rita Levi-Montalcini was 15 years old when Matteotti was murdered. The shocking news was a subject of much discussion in her household. At the same time, she recalled evidence in Turin of the rising power of the Fascist philosophy among certain Italian people. "The streets on the outskirts of town echoed in the evenings to the brazen and obscene chants of the Fascist gang-members," she wrote in her autobiography. She remembered hearing them cry, "'The gang of assassins are we! Long live Dumini! Long live Dumini!' The chants would continue with paeans to the Duce." [19] *Il Duce* (pronounced *eel DOO-chay* in Italian), or "the leader," was the nickname given in those early days to the rising Fascist leader, Mussolini. In the aftermath of Matteotti's murder, Benito Mussolini took control of Parliament and established himself as dictator of Italy.

Mussolini's swift rise to power had an instant and powerful effect on all Italians and especially on the lives of freethinking intellectuals like the Levi-Montalcinis. By November 1925, his government had banned all opposing political parties. No newspapers were allowed to criticize him or question the Fascist Party. "Thus began the repression of all those manifestations of cultural and intellectual life detested by the Fascist hierarchy and its followers," wrote Rita Levi-Montalcini years later, adding that the Fascists "were totally lacking in culture and always alert to the danger of a transgression." [20] Artists and scientists, professors and journalists, socialists and liberal thinkers alike began searching for ways to escape Mussolini's Italy. Those who remained lived in constant fear, not knowing what moves they might make that would be found offensive to the Fascist government and its vigilant police force. For Jewish Italians in particular, the rise of Mussolini meant repression. It would take a few more years until anti-Semitism truly overtook Italy, but events in Germany already provided stark signs of the direction in which things were headed.

A SCIENTIST, A JEW, AND A WOMAN: THREE COUNTS AGAINST HER

Rita Levi-Montalcini came of age during this period of instability and imminent terror in Italian politics. It was hard enough being a Jew and an intellectual, but added to that was the challenge of growing up in an age that still offered limited possibilities for women. Years later, as a

The Rise and Fall of Benito Mussolini

Benito Mussolini, born in 1883, began as a journalist, publishing a newspaper that argued that Italy should turn socialist, an ironic beginning for a man whose dictatorship attacked Italy's social revolutionaries. He often wrote that the workers of Italy should bind together like a *fascio,* or sheaf of wheat, an ancient Roman symbol for power. From that word, his political movement came to be called Fascism.

Fascism in Italy was a reactionary movement that rejected socialism and asserted the primary role of the state. It advocated an authoritarian government, one that enforced strong and sometimes oppressive measures against the population and exalted the nation above the individual.

When Mussolini was elected to parliament in 1921, the Fascist party was growing in strength. In October 1922 he threatened to overtake the king's government with his armed squads called the "Black Shirts." The frightened king appointed him prime minister, and he swiftly gained total control of the government. He named himself head of many different arms of the government, appointed all other leaders, took over the police and the military, and dictated the world-renowned scientist, Levi-Montalcini looked back, wryly using the language of genetics to describe the situation an ambitious young woman faced in the early twentieth century:

> Possessing two X chromosomes, it was my fate to grow to womanhood in a period when the natural intellectual faculties of an individual possessing an X and a Y—that is, a man—were reinforced rather than repressed. . . . a woman faced an almost insurmountable barrier if she wanted higher education and to realize her gifts. Though

way all laws should be written and enforced. His iron hand made it illegal for the people to question or criticize the Fascist regime.

Mussolini believed that Italy should conquer territory throughout the Mediterranean, and his imperial designs led to an alliance with Germany. Adolf Hitler's rise to power nearly paralleled Mussolini's. The two leaders became allied dictators, charged with a lust for power and a hatred for Jews, gypsies, and other social groups that they considered inferior.

Mussolini's leadership faltered during World War II. Following the landing of Allies in Sicily in 1943, his own followers turned against him. Italy became a battleground, invaded from the north by Germans and Austrians and attacked from the south and west by the British and Americans. Mussolini fled north, establishing a renegade government in the German-occupied area. Italians, with the support of the Allies, captured Mussolini in April 1945 and killed him and his mistress, ending the Fascist episode in Italian history.

the Victorian era passed away at the beginning of the twentieth century, its enduring influence on the kind of education given to young members of the two sexes continued to determine their roles. [21]

In Turin, the division between the genders started early in those days. From elementary school on, girls and boys attended different classes. Upon completion of the elementary grades, children entered a middle school, depending on the expectations of adults for their future. They could be channeled into schools that provided artistic or technical programs, that trained them to be elementary-level teachers, or that prepared them to attend a university. The latter was a choice virtually never offered to a girl. "Despite the fact that all three of us girls had demonstrated outstanding aptitude for study," wrote Levi-Montalcini of herself and her two sisters, "our father decided that we should attend middle school and then the girls' high school—from which, in those days, there was no possibility of going on to the university." [22] What that meant, in part, was that not one of the three Levi-Montalcini girls would be able to study mathematics and sciences, offered only in the high school for boys. Both Anna and Paola were content with the decision, interested as they were in writing and art. But Rita sensed that it was wrong for her, although she did not yet know why.

She had no artistic talents. In fact, she was not sure what talents she had. She had been given no education in the biological sciences, so she did not yet know how fascinating they could be to her. She thought she might study philosophy, but that was not offered in any high school classes. She read novels constantly, never cared about sports, and found herself filled with "a profound sense of isolation," part shyness and part conviction that she was not interested in a romantic relationship with a young man, which would simply lead her into the traditional female role of wife and mother. [23] As the

Levi-Montalcini children completed high school, Rita watched her sisters find paths that satisfied them. Anna found a husband, married, and then, in less than a year's time, gave birth to three children, including a set of twins. Paola became an apprentice in the studio of Felice Casorati, a well-known artist in Turin, and began painting in earnest. Meanwhile, recalled Rita, "I was asking myself how I was going to escape from the blind alley I seemed to be in." [24]

A DEVOTION TO FINDING A CURE

Fate provided an answer. Since before Rita and Paola's birth, a woman from the country named Giovanna Bruttata had lived with the Levi-Montalcini family, serving as governess to the children. At the time of the girls' high school graduation, Giovanna, only 45 years old, fell ill with cancer of the stomach. Her disease was diagnosed only after the malignant tumor had spread through and beyond her digestive system and had blocked her gastric tract. Giovanna came home to the Levi-Montalcinis, not really understanding the dire implications of her diagnosis. "I remember her thin and emaciated, sitting on a kitchen chair outlined against the gray sky of autumn," wrote Rita Levi-Montalcini years later, recognizing this moment as a turning point in her own life. "It was on that day that my decision took form, and I felt that I would be able to persuade Father. I would take up my studies again, and go into medicine." Grasping for any way to help her beloved governess avoid pain and death, Rita promised that "under my care she would certainly get well." [25] Giovanna Bruttata lived for only a few more months, but her illness aroused an ambition that propelled Rita Levi-Montalcini through the rest of her life.

> I told Mother of my decision to study medicine. She encouraged me to speak to Father. . . . I timidly asked if I might have a word with him after dinner . . . He said

I might have it there and then. I began in a roundabout way, telling him that, since I had no vocation for married life or for having babies, I would like to go back to studying. He listened, looking at me with that serious and penetrating gaze of his that caused me such trepidation, and asked whether I knew what I wanted to do. I told him how much Giovanna's death had shaken me and how I was convinced that the profession I wanted to follow was that of medical doctor. . . . He objected that it was a long and difficult course of study, unsuitable for a woman. . . . I assured him that I was not afraid of that.

Finally, she heard the answer that she wanted. "If this is really what you want," her freethinking father said to her, "then I won't stand in your way." [26]

Rita Levi-Montalcini had just turned 20. Just to get into medical school, she had to learn many new things, including Greek, Latin, and mathematics, which she either had never studied or else had not studied for many years. She convinced her cousin, Eugenia Lustig, to join her on this intellectual adventure. Together the two of them worked intensely, guided by tutors that their families hired for them. Finally, Rita Levi-Montalcini knew that she had found something that mattered to her. She and Eugenia both passed their entrance examinations and entered Turin's medical school, 2 of only 7 women among 300 first- and second-year students.

At the time, Rita Levi-Montalcini may have felt frustrated. She had to backtrack and resume her studies in order to catch up with the young men who had moved straight through from high school to medical school. But years later, she thanked her father for making decisions that prolonged the time it took her to choose her career. "If I had studied classics after middle school, as had been my wish, I would certainly have enrolled in philosophy," she wrote. [27] By delaying her decision and extending her program of study through her teenage years, Rita Levi-Montalcini came to make the decision of her lifetime. She turned her attention toward medicine, and found in that new goal "the very reason of my existence." [28]

3 A Budding Scientist

1930–1934

WORKING FOR THE MASTER ANATOMIST

In the fall of 1930, for the first of many times, Rita Levi-Montalcini went to class in what she called "the somber and stately amphitheater of the Institute of Anatomy of the Turin School of Medicine." [29] Her major professor was Giuseppe Levi, a tall, robust anatomist with a deep baritone voice, known for flying into a rage when students did not quiet down as he entered the room. His thick red hair and bushy eyebrows earned him the nickname of "Levipom," a combination of his name and a syllable from the Italian word for tomato, *pomodoro*. Like Levi-Montalcini, Giuseppe Levi was Jewish; like her father, he was an intellectual, a freethinker, and passionately anti-Fascist. He did not mince words, and he often harangued friends about the wrongdoings of *il Duce* and his followers. He was demanding and judgmental as a teacher, dismissive to those students who didn't learn quickly, but absolutely devoted to those who proved their worth. He would stand in the middle of the amphitheater, booming out to his medical students the anatomical lessons they were to be learning, waving his bamboo cane toward the blackboard and then at body parts of the cadaver laid out on the table before him.

Both Rita and her cousin Eugenia passed first-year exams with honors, and Professor Levi appointed them laboratory interns. The study of anatomy did not particularly interest Levi-Montalcini, but working more closely with the extraordinary Professor Giuseppe Levi did. [30] His research specialty was the way cells grow in the nervous system. At the time that Levi-Montalcini began working for him, he was analyzing the patterns of cell growth in the nervous systems of mice, and he considered it important to compare nerve systems cells among many different mice, to see how much variation in pattern there was between one individual and another. He assigned his interns to prepare histology, or tissue, samples on slides for observation under the microscope. They had to cut out bits of brain or spinal cord from many lab mice, making slices so thin that single cells could be viewed under the microscope.

"Half a century ago, at the time of my internship, histology was more of an art than a science, lacking the highly elaborate techniques available today," Levi-Montalcini wrote in her autobiography in 1988, looking back over six decades of laboratory technology.

> With the techniques then at our disposal, the best among us would obtain satisfactory results in the preparation of tissues from laboratory animals, from biopsy or autopsy. These preparations consisted of slices a few microns thick (a micron is one thousandth of a millimeter), fixed, stained, carefully arranged on glass slides, and examined through an optical microscope. This microscope was improved but not essentially different in construction from the first such microscope used around 1660 by the great Bolognese biologist Marcello Malpighi for studying the structure of vegetable and animal tissues. [31]

Such delicate procedures did not come easily to Levi-Montalcini, but over the course of the next few months, she became especially good at performing one procedure: silver impregnation of tissues. When silver nitrate is infused into nerve cell samples, certain important features absorb the stain, while others do not, making it easier to distinguish between cells in the tissue. In Levi's research, the stain accentuated the sensory ganglia, oval-shaped cells branching off the spinal column that are responsible for the transmission of sensory information between the brain and all parts of the body.

It was tedious work to count the cells in slide after slide of mouse nerve tissue. Some of the interns just made up the

The Early Exploration of Nerve Cells

In the 1830s, using primitive microscopes, scientists viewed nerve cells and saw two basic shapes: ovals or teardrops and long fibers. What the relationship was between the two shapes, no one could determine until two European anatomists, Camillo Golgi from Italy and Santiago Ramón y Cajal from Spain, developed ways to infuse tiny amounts of stains into cells and highlight their interiors.

Golgi invented a staining technique using a combination of silver nitrate and potassium dichromate, which in reaction had the effect of giving dark outlines to the working parts of nerve cells. Details inside cells showed forth under a microscope as never before.

Ramón y Cajal, considered by many to be the greatest neuroanatomist of the nineteenth century, improved on Golgi's staining techniques. Then, based on diligent slide preparations over many years, he created intricate and delicate drawings of many parts of the nervous system. Through these meticulous observations, he determined three basic rules of every nervous system. First, the neuron is the basic cellular unit of the nervous system. Second, a neuron has three parts: the soma or cell body, the dendrites, and the axon, which branches at the end. Third, signals come in through the dendrites, enter the cell body, and travel out the branching ends of the axon toward other cells. Ramón y Cajal's observations pointed the way toward understanding the function of nerve synapses, the meeting points where one nerve communicates with another.

For their distinguished work in neuroanatomy, Golgi and Ramón y Cajal together received the Nobel Prize in Medicine or Physiology in 1906. Oddly enough, the two men argued certain points of interpretation in their acceptance speeches. Ultimately, Ramón y Cajal's hypothesis of how nerve cells worked together proved the more accurate picture.

numbers. A visiting professor privately told Levi-Montalcini he thought it was a useless effort. Even she had her doubts—Could anyone reliably count hundreds of cells clustered under a microscope?—but she performed the task as well as she could. Years later, she looked back and recognized the value of the work Levi set her and other medical students to doing. The experiment wasn't just a matter of counting, she wrote in her autobiography. "Its aim, in fact, was to determine whether the number of cells in specific and clearly identifiable nervous groupings is rigidly fixed and not subject to fluctuations as a result of environmental factors." [32] Levi was ahead of his time, in fact, but he did not have the equipment or techniques to perfect his work. Neuroscientists are still asking the same basic question today, and in fact that very question was to stand at the heart of the science that won Rita Levi-Montalcini the Nobel Prize more than half a century later.

Eventually Professor Levi assigned Rita Levi-Montalcini another project: to study how convolutions in the brain form as the human fetus develops. From the start, Levi-Montalcini considered it "a task destined to total failure." [33] How could she ever obtain the subjects from which to prepare laboratory slides? Abortions were illegal, so the only way she could get tissue to study was to request that hospitals provide her fetuses expelled by miscarriage. Her research went poorly, drawing the criticism of "the Master" and making even her doubt her own capabilities as a scientist. It was a hard time for her emotionally, and then she fell ill. Needing surgery, she had to leave school and the research lab for a month. She felt gratified the day Giuseppe Levi came to visit her in the hospital. It helped her understand that despite her current research troubles, he respected and cared for her. When she returned to work at the medical school, she was thankful to learn that Professor Levi had assigned her to a different project.

This time, she would help him with his *in vitro* nerve cell studies, studies of cells removed from their biological source and placed in sterile laboratory dishes in a medium that would keep them alive and growing. Eugenia and Rita worked together exploring the nervous system's reticular fibers, branching fibers that weave through an entire system composing, in Levi-Montalcini's words, "the weft that supports the complex of tissues of which they are a part." [34] While it had been believed that these fibers form only in connective tissue such as bones and cartilage, the two students used silver staining techniques to demonstrate that they are also produced by special cells found in muscle and epithelium, or lining, tissue as well. These findings were significant enough that both women used the work as the basis of their doctoral theses.

THE DEATH OF HER FATHER

At the end her second year of medical school, Rita Levi-Montalcini's father suffered a series of strokes. "Coming home late one afternoon," she recalled in her autobiography, "I was surprised to find him sitting on the dining-room balcony, so lost in thought as not to notice my presence or my greeting." [35] Her mother told her that while at work, he had found himself unable to find the right words. Difficulty in talking, they all knew, was likely a sign of a stroke, an obstruction of blood flowing into a certain part of his brain. The symptoms disappeared, but clearly Adamo Levi-Montalcini was worried. He put on a positive face for his family and refused to slow down in his work at all. He would ride the trolley half an hour to his factory, outside of town, trying to ignore the pains of angina—constrictions in the chest caused by a lack of oxygen flow to the heart, a precursor to a heart attack— that he was feeling more and more often. Only months later did those who worked with him at the factory tell his

The Basic Shape of Nerve Cells

The basic structure of neurons was well known by the time that Rita Levi-Montalcini embarked on her studies of the nervous system. Neurons contain three parts: (1) the soma, or cell body, (2) the axon, or sending nerve fiber, and (3) the dendrites, or receiving nerve fibers. Messages travel throughout the nervous system by means of impulse transmissions down the axons and tiny chemical transmissions going from neuron to neuron. The brain and spinal column are the central organs of this vast circuit. Signals come to and from the brain, through the spinal cord, then out and down into the body's organs and extremities.

The soma is the central part of the nerve cell. Signals come into the soma through the cell's many dendrites, which branch out at the tips and receive transmissions from nearby cells. This multitude of signals is collected and summed up in the soma. Then, in a flash, a responding impulse goes from the soma, out the axon, to the dendrites of other cells. Axons usually branch out at their tips, as dendrites do, creating communication pathways with numerous other cells. Under a microscope, the end of each axon fiber looks like a little knob. Called a synaptic terminal, the cell ending is designed as nozzle through which minute bundles of chemicals are released and transferred across a junction, the synapse, onto receiving dendrites.

This transfer of chemicals goes on continuously in the nervous system of every living thing. It has been calculated that a chemical signal moves into, through, and out of a typical neuron at a speed of about 200 miles per hour. Considering that there are as many as 10,000,000,000 neurons in the human body, that's a lot of nerve impulses whizzing around without your even knowing it.

wife how often he would hold his hand to his chest and slump over while he was there.

On July 30, 1932, Adamo Levi-Montalcini experienced another attack in the middle of the night. His wife called their daughter, the soon-to-be doctor, to ask what to do. They administered nitroglycerine, a treatment that widens the arteries and increases blood flow to the heart. Rita was relieved to find her father awake and cheerful in the morning, saying he felt fine. Two days later, though, attacks were coming more frequently, with pain all up and down the right side of his body. "What turned out to be the final attack began at seven in the evening, his favorite time of day, which he loved to spend in contemplation of the swallows in flight," his daughter remembered many years later. She remembers hearing him say to himself, after several of the attacks, "And afterward?" The freethinker had no religious visions of heaven with which to answer that question. [36]

His wife, all four of his children, and his three grandchildren were at his bedside when Adamo Levi-Montalcini died.

> I can still see Paola kneeling at his side, overcome with emotion, her eyes filled with tears, as she desperately rubbed a hot soaking towel on his legs and feet. And I can see Father's expression as, with infinite tenderness, he stroked her hair. . . . We eased him onto the bed and, holding one another, watched his life slowly fade away. It was six o'clock on that summer morning, and the clear light of dawn lit up his face and ours, which were paler than the one lying on the pillow. I kissed his forehead, cold and still damp with the sweat of his final struggle, and thought with anguish of the kisses I had been unable to give him in my childhood. [37]

The shock of her father's death left Rita Levi-Montalcini distraught, but in the long run she realized that he died with the same intensity as he had lived. She regretted that theirs had not been a warmer, more demonstrative relationship. Maybe she should have kissed him more often, mustache and all. But she felt serene, knowing that she could thank him for so many of the features in her character that made her who she was, that day and for the life to come: her dedication to hard work, her passion for the world of ideas, and her ability to be a freethinker, not only in the realm of religion but also in politics, science, and the ways she chose to live her life.

Scenes from the Life of Rita Levi-Montalcini

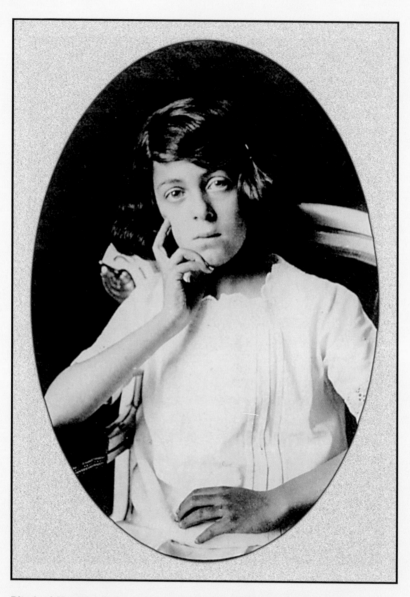

Rita Levi-Montalcini, as a young girl (age 11) in Turin, Italy. The melancholy stare of her gray-green eyes, according to her mother, came from her maternal grandmother, whom she was thought to resemble closely. Rita was a deeply sensitive child who feared the dark and shunned physical contact with others (and especially avoided kissing her father's mustached face!). Her twin sister, Paola, a happy-go-lucky child with an artistic bent, did not share these somber traits.

Adamo Levi and Adele Montalcini in 1905, with their two oldest children, Anna (left) and Gino (right). In 1909, twins Rita and Paola were born to the Levi-Montalcinis. The family was of Jewish ancestry, although Adamo, a liberal freethinker, instructed his children to respond "freethinker" when pressed for their religious affiliation. In deference to the more traditional Adele, Adamo agreed to participate in certain Jewish celebrations.

Rita (left) and Paola Levi-Montalcini, in the forest at Forte dei Marmi, Italy, in 1938. It was at this time that Mussolini, dictator of Italy, and his anti-Semitic agenda, forbade Jews such as Rita from teaching or researching publicly and from publishing articles in scientific journals. These laws eventually forced her to do her research "underground."

Turin, Italy, around 1900. The view here is from the Mount of the Capuchins. A northern industrial center, it was occupied by the Nazis during World War II. Rita loved her beautiful hometown and loathed the destruction caused there by Allied bombings and by the retreating Germans.

Santiago Ramón y Cajal (1852–1934), a pioneer in neuroembryology who developed state-of-the art staining techniques and proposed the cellular structure of the central nervous system, which eventually earned him a Nobel Prize in 1906. His work greatly influenced the young Rita Levi-Montalcini.

Viktor Hamburger, a neurobiologist and pupil of Nobel Prize–winner Hans Spemann. One of Hamburger's papers, published in an American journal, caused Levi-Montalcini to pursue similar research with chick embryos in a clandestine laboratory set up in her bedroom, since the Nazis forbade Jewish scientists from research. Hamburger eventually invited Levi-Montalcini to join his research team at Washington University, in St. Louis.

Rebstock Hall, on the Washington University campus, in St. Louis. It is here that Levi-Montalcini met and worked with Stanley Cohen on their theory of the nerve growth factor (NGF), which eventually earned them the Nobel Prize in 1986. This photo shows the building as it looked in the 1980s.

Rita Levi-Montalcini in her Washington University laboratory, 1959. The groundbreaking neuroembryological research that Levi-Montalcini and Stanley Cohen carried out in the winter of 1958 and the spring of 1959 was done with the help of newborn mice.

Stanley Cohen in his lab at Vanderbilt University in 1986. Cohen worked with Levi-Montalcini at Washington University until budget cuts at the university in 1959 eliminated the possibility that Cohen could be offered a full-time staff position there. In this photo, Cohen has just learned that he and Levi-Montalcini will receive the 1986 Nobel Prize in Medicine.

Rita Levi-Montalcini, receiving the 1986 Nobel Prize in Medicine from the King of Sweden. Levi-Montalcini had traveled far—from her childhood in Turin, Italy, as a shy child, afraid of the dark, to an American scientist receiving a Nobel Prize. Her groundbreaking work in neuroembryology, the early parts of which were carried on in secret in Fascist Italy, spanned two continents and a half century.

4

Suppressed Science in a Fascist Regime

1935–1945

THE GROWING THREAT OF FASCISM

For most of Rita Levi-Montalcini's life, war, unrest, and struggles for power rocked her homeland. She was a first-grade student in 1915 when Italy entered World War I. Elsewhere in Europe, fighting had been going on for nearly a year. A Serbian plot to gain independence from the Austro-Hungarian Empire quickly exploded into a war among nations as Germany sided with Austro-Hungary and Russia sided with Serbia. (For more information on this period, enter "Serbian plot, 1914" into a search engine and browse the sites listed.) Italy, since 1882 in a Triple Alliance with Germany and Austro-Hungary, at first declared that it would remain neutral. France and Britain took up arms, aligning with Russia and Serbia, as Germany invaded Belgium. Austrian troop movements to the south and west threatened Italian territories. In secret negotiations, Italian ministers agreed to join the Allied forces of France, Britain, and Russia. Italian soldiers stood guard at their country's border with Austro-Hungary until the war ended in 1918.

For a first-grade student, that war was at once distant, 300 hundred miles and a vast mountain range away, yet ever-present. Rita's most vivid memories of the war spirit were embodied in her beloved schoolteacher, a patriotic woman who revered King Umberto II and Queen Maria José, the royal leaders of Italy. Sometimes her teacher's elder sister, a Red Cross war nurse, would visit the classroom. "Her white uniform with its large red cross, and her devotion to the cause . . . filled me with enthusiasm," recalled Levi-Montalcini. [38] In her childish way, she hoped the war would last long enough that she, too, could wear such a uniform and provide valuable service on the battlefield. When the war did come to an end, she and her fellow fourth-graders were assigned to memorize the Italian general's proud public statement: "The enemy are in rout and, with our victorious troops in hot pursuit, are fleeing hopelessly and in disorder back through the valleys from which they came down with such arrogant confidence four years ago." [39]

While they did not directly affect Rita Levi-Montalcini as she moved through high school and into the university, Italian politics remained unsettled. For many Italians, issues at home were more important than issues among other nations of Europe. Factory workers, supported by members of Italy's Socialist Party, were demanding better pay and work conditions. A new political party came into being soon after the end of World War I, created in large part by a journalist named Benito Mussolini. Out of his writing, ideas, and leadership grew the Italian Fascist Party. The struggle between the Fascists and the Socialists, both of whom wanted to take control of the country, grew more and more violent. In 1922, King Umberto II named Mussolini his prime minister, which marked the beginning of the Fascist party's successful rise to power in Italy.

ANTI-SEMITISM BECOMES THE LAW

At first, Italians saw Mussolini as a hero, someone who would move Italy into the future and improve conditions for the working class. As his grasp on power grew, though, Mussolini's vision changed character. His government took on the ironclad character of a dictatorship, passing laws that demanded obedience and taking strict, sometimes violent, action against any person or organization that threatened it. Meanwhile, Adolf Hitler had come to power in Germany in 1933, and the two leaders allied in support of General Francisco Franco and rebel forces in the Spanish Civil War, starting in 1936.

A racial agenda stood at the heart of Hitler's government. He believed that Germany should become a purely Aryan nation. The word "Aryan" referred to people of fair-skinned, Northern European stock, but in Hitler's Germany, it especially came to mean "not Jewish." The quest for a pure Aryan nation turned into the horrific extermination of the Jewish people in Germany and other countries that either collaborated with Germany or were invaded by it. During the late 1930s,

Mussolini's government began promoting the same vicious attitudes and actions. In private, few Italians agreed or cooperated with anti-Semitic efforts. The late 1930s and 1940s were a time of anxiety and fear for Italian Jews, but many found friendship, support, and even hiding places among their non-Jewish friends and neighbors.

From 1938 on, anti-Semitic messages appeared more and more frequently in Italy's newspapers. Mussolini's government laid down racial laws that restricted the rights, movement, and power of all Jews in Italy. Public announcements were made that in essence stated that no Jew could rightfully call himself or herself Italian. Jewish intellectuals were banned from studying or teaching in Italian universities. Intellectuals in general were considered a threat, their activities restricted. On October 16, 1938, the government decreed that anyone Jewish was "suspended from academic work and from all posts in the universities and academies." [40] Responding with what her friends called "dangerous outrage and impetuousness," [41] Levi-Montalcini spoke even more proudly of her Jewish identity. "The monster of anti-Semitism, all the more menacing for being invisible and yet ever present, had come out of its lair; the ungraspable phantom had become an actual and tangible reality," she wrote half a century later. "I felt pride in being Jewish . . . and, though still profoundly secular, I felt a bond with those who were, like me, the victims of the lurid campaign unleashed by the Fascist press." [42] It became more obvious, as the months went by, that the Fascist secret police were planting informers everywhere, including in the university classrooms and labs. Rita Levi-Montalcini, just beginning to forge her own path in the field of neuroscience, finally had to give up something so close to her heart, it was like losing her life: She had to abandon her work in the laboratory.

It was the wrong time to stop her research. She was collaborating with a research assistant, Fabio Visintini, using new techniques to understand growth patterns in the nervous systems of chick embryos. Visintini had perfected a way to implant electrodes on key nerve sites within the growing

The Body's Nervous System

The nervous system works because millions of neurons, or nerve cells, transmit and receive signals all the time, spreading impulses between the brain, the spinal column, and every part of the body: the parts that sense, the parts that move, and the parts that function without conscious control, like the organs of digestion, respiration, and circulation.

The spinal column plays the central role of traffic control in this vast network of nerve impulses. A sensation, such as the feeling of a fingertip touching a hot stove, travels by chemical messengers moving up a pathway of sensory neurons through the finger, arm, and shoulder, into the area of the spinal cord dedicated to that part of the body, then up the spine and into the brain. A motion, such as the deliberate pluck of a guitar string by a fingertip, occurs when similar chemical messengers travel, neuron to neuron, out from the brain, through the spinal column down a pathway of motor neurons into the muscle groups that will move your finger, arm, and shoulder in the direction needed to play that note.

Amazingly enough, a single nerve cell can measure a foot or more in length. There are neurons with a cell body in the brain whose axons, or transmitting cell parts, reach from inside the skull to the base of the spine, or from the spinal column all the way down to the toe. Consider how long the axons must be for the neurons that transmit impulses from the brain to the legs of a giraffe. In that case, the cell's soma is in the skull, and the same cell's axon is long enough to reach from the giraffe's head all the way to the end of its spinal column, which serves the animal's hindquarters.

embryo. Those electrodes were wired to an oscilloscope, which graphed out the signals they sensed. As nerve impulses occurred within the embryo, they translated into light blips on a screen. By tracking the impulses in the same growing embryo over many days, Visintini could create a representation through time of changing electrical impulses occurring in its nervous system. Simultaneously, Levi-Montalcini was viewing tissue sections, stained with silver, that corresponded with each phase of measurements her laboratory partner was taking. Their work together created a fuller picture of embryonic nervous system development, combining observations about the chick embryo's morphology (systems and patterns of cells), electrophysiology (electrical charges in the body), and behavior (especially the ability to move and to sense things). Hundreds of papers later, two years after winning the Nobel Prize, Levi-Montalcini considered the paper that she wrote based on these experiments "one of my most rewarding."[43] No Italian journal would publish it, though, because one of the authors was Jewish. A year later, it was translated into French and published in a little-known Belgian journal, *Archive de Biologie.*

FLEEING THE FASCIST THREAT

Politically, things in Italy got markedly worse. "By March 1939," Rita Levi-Montalcini recalled, "I could no longer attend university institutes without risking denunciation or endangering Aryan friends," who would themselves be seen as enemies of the government if they showed any sympathy toward the Jews they knew.[44] When an invitation came to her from the director of a neurological institute in Brussels, Belgium, to come and work there, Rita Levi-Montalcini accepted, pleased to move to the same country where both her older sister, with her family, and her favorite professor, Giuseppe Levi, had already moved. Every weekend, she would travel from Brussels, the capital of Belgium, to Liège, a city 50 miles to the east, to spend the day talking about her work and ideas with Professor Levi. This routine, although not as rewarding as working at home, satisfied Rita Levi-Montalcini's need to continue her research. She lived in Belgium for only part of a year, from the spring through the fall of 1939, for the news of Germany's invasion into Poland heightened fears across all Europe and especially among European Jews. She and her family decided that Italy, still politically neutral, might be safer than Belgium. They returned to Turin, then soon fled into the countryside nearby, where Levi-Montalcini did her best to continue her neuroscientific investigations on chicken eggs bought from farms nearby.

Despite the "Pact of Steel" that Italy had signed with Germany in August 1939, allying the two countries, Mussolini kept his nation "nonbelligerent" during the first year of World War II. Historians believe that he wanted to be sure he sided with the winner. (For more information on this alliance, enter "Pact of Steel, 1839" into a search engine and browse the sites listed.) In the first months of 1940, Nazi troops invaded Denmark, Norway, France, Belgium, Luxembourg, the Netherlands, and, finally, France. As they occupied Paris in June 1940, Mussolini declared war on France and its ally, Great Britain. Soviet Russian troops advanced on new territory in Eastern Europe. Battles occurred in the Mediterranean and northern Africa as well. Italy, strategically positioned between the two theaters of war, felt the pressure of invasion coming from both directions, as German tanks advanced from the north and British pilots, joined by Americans from 1941 on, attacked from the south.

In 1943, the Levi-Montalcini family faced a dilemma. As the Allies invaded Italy, German tanks had rolled into their home city of Turin, and all of northern Italy had been ceded by the Fascists to the Nazis. A Jewish family like theirs had three choices. They could stay in their beloved Piedmont region, now under the rule of the Germans. They could, like the royal family and many others fearful of the Fascists, flee to southern Italy, in the hopes that the Allies would advance and take possession of that territory. Or they could cross the mountains into Switzerland, which remained neutral throughout the war. They tried the third alternative, but

Primo Levi: Chemist, Author, and Survivor

Some Italian Jews were captured and sent to German death camps. One such man was Primo Levi.

Levi was 10 years younger than Rita Levi-Montalcini (and not related to her or to her professor) but, like her, he studied science at the University of Turin during the years when anti-Semitism was on the rise in Italy. In 1944, two years after his graduation, because of his contacts with groups resisting the Fascist regime, Levi was captured and ultimately sent to Auschwitz, Germany's most notorious death camp. He survived, but he was haunted through the rest of his life by his memories and guilt over being one of the few who lived. After World War II, he returned to Turin and to his profession as a chemist, developing a manufacturing process for varnishing copper wire.

From his holocaust memories, Levi wrote fiction, nonfiction, and poems. In his first book, *This Is a Man,* he chronicled what he saw, thought, and was made to do in the concentration camp. In his novel *If Not Now, When?* he told the story of a group of Jewish refugees who travel from Russia to Italy, hoping ultimately to reach the Holy Land in the Middle East. His book of essays, *Other People's Trades,* included a list of reasons why someone like him would write, which included "To teach something to someone," "To improve the world," and "To free oneself from anguish."

Primo Levi died in 1987, falling over a railing down three flights of stairs. Many believe it was suicide. He meant so much to Rita Levi-Montalcini that she ended her own autobiography, which she was writing at the time he died, with an epilogue addressed to him, thanking him for being one of those who "kept alive the fire of hope" for others.

border police stopped them and forced them to take a train south. Instead of returning to Turin, they went to Florence, further south, in the center of the Italian peninsula. They contacted a dear friend of Paola's, who helped them find a place to stay. It was late 1943.

Politics in Rome had become more complicated and chaotic. Largely because of military defeats, Benito Mussolini swiftly lost his following. On July 25, 1943, all Italy heard the news that he had resigned, replaced as head of government by Pietro Badoglio. Badoglio immediately began negotiations with the Allies, signaling his country's refusal to cooperate with the Nazis anymore. For a moment, some Italians felt hope, but none of the Jews that Levi-Montalcini knew allowed themselves that luxury. They were skeptical that things could improve so quickly. Hitler still held massive power. Italians who thought their problems were solved by the disappearance of Mussolini were displaying an "irresponsible attitude," Levi-Montalcini and her friends believed, built on the false faith that by hating the Nazis, all Italians would unite and become immune to the horrors and devastation still going on elsewhere in Europe. It was an attitude, Levi-Montalcini sadly wrote years later, "which was to cause thousands of people untold suffering and death."[45] In fact, now Germany had all the more reason to invade Italy from the north.

In October 1943, Italy declared war on Germany. For the next 18 months, until the end of World War II, Italy became a theater of war.

SECRET SCIENCE

In these days of chaos and destruction, Rita Levi-Montalcini preserved herself as well as she could by continuing to focus her mind on her science. She had hoped to be able to continue her research at the University of Florence, but Jews were still not allowed in Italy's schools or institutions. The very idea "alarmed the director of the Neurological Institute, who said that there was no way for me to attend it 'incognito,'" [46] recalled Levi-Montalcini. Frustrated, she did what she could to read and keep up with the work of others, and was delighted one spring day in 1944 when her doorbell rang and "I recognized the imperious voice of Professor Levi asking for me." Thanks to his son, who had long before proved himself capable of brave acts in the face of danger, Levi had escaped from the wartorn Piedmont and was living in Florence under a more Italian-sounding name: Lovisato.

Master and student resumed work together, this time revising a two-volume textbook on histology that Levi had drafted. Often, Levi retreated to the safer countryside to stay with his daughter. That is where he was when, on August 3, 1944, the sirens of Florence blared out, signaling a state of emergency. Always dedicated to the pursuit of knowledge, Rita Levi-Montalcini fled through the streets of Florence, risking her life to reach Levi's apartment and rescue the massive manuscript from possible destruction. That night she lay awake, listening as mines planted by the Nazis blew up Florence's bridges, ancient architectural masterpieces that had spanned the Arno River for centuries.

In a state of emergency, no one in Florence could expect electricity, bread, or water. All they knew of what was going on was the news they could glean from neighbors they dared to talk with. Would this condition of life last another week, another month, another year? No one knew.

Hope rekindled in early September.

On 2 September, the British marched silently [through Florence] along the streets packed with onlookers. For the first time I saw, after the soldiers had passed, a bus marked with a Star of David—now no longer an object of derision. Water tanks bearing the emblem were going around distributing water to the thirsty population. [47]

Now, no longer fearful to present the ID cards that declared them Jewish, the Levi-Montalcinis and thousands of others could receive rations. It was the beginning of the liberation.

CARING FOR THOSE WHO NEED HER

For much of the next year, Rita Levi-Montalcini found herself in a position to do what she had long ago dreamed of doing: providing medical care to the needy in a wartime setting. "At the beginning of September 1944, I presented myself to the Allies' health service," she wrote, "and was assigned, along with three other doctors, to what was to be my most intense, most exhausting, and final experience as a medical doctor."[48] Fighting continued through the mountainous region that forms the north-central backbone of Italy. Allied trucks carried refugees from the front back to Florence. Levi-Montalcini and others tended their injuries in the many buildings commandeered as army hospitals. Hers was an old military barracks, recently used as a stable and soldiers' dormitory. Straw still covered the earthen floor and stuffed the patient mattresses.

"I dedicated myself with enthusiasm to the double [role] of doctor and nurse," wrote Levi-Montalcini. Each night, trucks brought more refugees into the barracks.

> My duty was to see that their state of health was checked and then that they were settled somewhere in the shed. The consequences of malnutrition and of the cold were particularly evident in babies and old people. I had never in the course of my brief experience as a practicing physician . . . witnessed a sight so painful. Many of the newborn children arrived in a state of extreme dehydration. At dawn I would take them to the pediatric clinic, only to be an impotent witness to the extinguishing of the lives of those small creatures, by then already on the threshold of death.[49]

An epidemic of typhoid swept through the infirmary, and the uneducated patients often blamed their nurses and doctors for the illness and death they witnessed all around them. The medical caregivers, though, knowing full well that they were equally at risk for the vicious disease, stayed dedicated to their work. These months left Rita Levi-Montalcini with faces floating in her memory: those of the people she cared for whom she could not keep from dying.

The typhoid epidemic lessened in April 1945. As if in harmony, the Nazi threat weakened at the same time. Allied troops, joined by Italians, fought together to weaken the German stronghold in the north. On April 28, Italian soldiers captured and executed Benito Mussolini, who was trying to escape in secret to Switzerland. They photographed his dead body for all Italians to see, then carried it to Rome for public display. Two days later, Adolf Hitler committed suicide. On May 8, 1945, a victory for the Allies was declared in Europe. World War II was not yet over, for aggression between the United States and Japan was still underway in the Pacific. But for the Jews in Italy, the worst of the suffering was behind them. For Rita Levi-Montalcini, it was time to get back to work in the neuroscience laboratory.

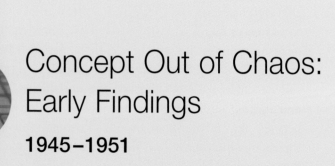

Concept Out of Chaos:
Early Findings

1945–1951

5

AN INVITATION TO AMERICA

In the summer of 1945, Rita Levi-Montalcini and her family returned to Turin. The dictatorship of Mussolini and the war in Europe were over, but their beloved city did not feel the same. "It was not easy to resume the rhythms of a life so brutally interrupted by the storm of war," Levi-Montalcini wrote in her autobiography. "With the disappearance of the danger that had threatened the survival of many of us, so also disappeared the strength or blind daring that enables one to overcome life's most difficult moments." [50] True to form, she overcame her depression by focusing on her scientific work. Giuseppe Levi was back in his laboratory, where she started working as well, still trying to perfect the techniques of impregnating nerve cells in developing embryos with silver stains to view their patterns more clearly.

Then came a letter that would change Rita Levi-Montalcini's life. "On a summer day in 1946, Levi called me into his study and showed me a letter dated 8 July he had just received from Professor Viktor Hamburger, chairman of the department of zoology at Washington University in St. Louis." [51] Levi-Montalcini knew well the work of Viktor Hamburger. His was the paper that had so inspired her in 1940, as she rode in the cattle car, smelling fresh hay and watching the Italian landscape go by. Hamburger's paper on chick embryo system development dated from 1934. The problem still fascinated him, and, being a diligent and omnivorous scholar, he had read Levi-Montalcini's 1943 paper about her work with Visintini in the Belgian biology journal.

Hamburger wrote Levi because, as Levi-Montalcini explained it, "he was curious about my conclusions regarding the mechanisms governing the effects of peripheral tissues on the development of the nervous fibers that innervate them—conclusions completely different from his own." [52] Both studies had asked how it happens that nerve cells in the core of the embryo change their pattern of growth in response to a change on the periphery, or outer edge, of the embryo. Both scientists had noted, specifically, that when a chick embryo loses a wing bud, the nerve section in the spine that would have served that wing shrinks almost immediately. Hamburger suggested that impulses traveled from the wing area back to the spinal cord, moving along the most primitive of nerve fibers. Levi-Montalcini found that nerves in the spinal area begin to form as if they were needed to serve the wing, but then those cells start dying. It was a subtle point, but it made a big difference in the larger scheme of things. Embryologists seek to describe every step and detail in the story of how a tiny cluster of cells multiplies and organizes itself, how every cell and group of cells takes on a distinctive assignment, ultimately coordinating into the complex workings of a mature living being. In the case of the week-old chick embryo, did the growing wing area direct the pattern of nerve cells as they grew into it, or were the cells inside the spinal cord already programmed to become the wing's nervous system?

Viktor Hamburger wanted to work on these questions in his St. Louis laboratory, and he wanted Rita Levi-Montalcini to work on them with him. He invited her to join the Washington University faculty for a year, beginning in the fall semester of 1947. As it happened, she would continue working at Washington University in St. Louis for the next three momentous decades.

A NEW VIEW OF NERVE CELLS

Viktor Hamburger proved to be entirely different than the abrasive Giuseppe Levi, with whom Rita Levi-Montalcini had grown accustomed to working. In the late 1940s, Hamburger was already recognized as a leader in experimental neurobiology, and yet he was humble, tolerant, and respectful of those who worked under him. "I was struck by the kindness and subtle dry humor of Viktor, who would never hurt other people's feelings nor show his disagreement with more than a few gentle remarks and a firm glance of disapproval," Levi-Montalcini recalled. [53] The atmosphere of an American university was also very different from anything she had previously known.

Although the discoveries of science, when retold, seem exciting, the daily routine of a scientist can be boring. For months, Levi-Montalcini prepared slides with tiny bits of tissue, staining them carefully with the silver nitrate that helped define certain cells, then viewing them under the microscope and, when the findings had any inkling of significance, making careful drawings of what she saw. For months, she privately wondered whether there was much hope of finding anything important in her observations of nervous system development. Occasionally she would spend a weekend traveling to Bloomington, Indiana, where two of her university friends, Salvador Luria and Renato Dulbecco, now worked in science laboratories as well. She looked with envy on Luria's work in microbiology, thinking he was probably headed for more important findings than she would ever reach. (For more information on this important scientist, enter "Salvador Luria" into a search engine and browse the sites listed.)

Then, one day, routinely proceeding through her daily laboratory regimen, she noticed a pattern among the nerve cells she was viewing. Something clicked. A new idea developed. Suddenly she saw her object of study differently.

It happened in the course of one afternoon in late autumn of 1947, while I was somewhat haphazardly examining, under the microscope, the latest series of silver-salt–impregnated chick-embryo sections. Their coloring had come out perfectly: the nerve cells that had begun to differentiate in the cerebral vesicles and spinal cord . . . stood out in their every detail with a deep brown-blackish hue on the golden yellow background of the nonimpregnated cord tissue formed of satellite cells and as yet undifferentiated nerve cells. . . . The thoracic and sacral segments offered a spectacle not unlike that of the maneuvers of large armies on a battlefield. Thousands of cells in the thoracic segment, and a smaller number in the sacral one, were proceeding in long columns . . . of the spinal cord. [54]

Noting what seemed to her, as she put it, an example of "migration" in the developing system of cells, she compared it in her mind to the way that birds, termites, or ants "migrate," that is, instinctually travel in formation together,

The Long Life and Important Work of Viktor Hamburger

Viktor Hamburger was born in 1900 in a small Prussian town in a region now part of Poland. His passion for biology began when he was just a child. He fought in World War I, then studied at the University of Heidelberg in Germany, where he became fascinated with the study of embryology, the first stages of life from conception to birth. He became the student of Hans Spemann, who won the Nobel Prize in 1935 for his discovery, using the large eggs of amphibians, that certain cells perform an organizing function in embryos.

Hamburger was studying for a year in Chicago when the Nazi regime of Germany ejected all Jews from the universities. A Jew himself, he chose to stay in the United States, joining the faculty of Washington University in St. Louis, Missouri. He worked there for 65 years, and he was chairman of the department of zoology for 35.

In Spemann's laboratory, Hamburger had worked on amphibian embryos. He decided to try chick embryos heading together for the same destination. Maybe the concept of "instinct," an inborn drive inside an animal, could not be applied to cells, since animals have the mental capability to make decisions. But cells did behave, it appeared, according to a "program" inside them, something not that different from what we call instinct in an animal. "That day," Levi-Montalcini recalled, "as I peered through the microscope, nerve cells were acquiring a personality not usually attributed to them." [55]

Looking more closely at what was happening at the cellular level, Levi-Montalcini found herself using the metaphor of bodies on a battlefield. She observed how, as a community of cells developed, one could lose its outer

instead, since their nerve centers were even more clearly visible under the microscope. He figured out how to saw a tiny hole into an eggshell and, using a glass microneedle, perform surgery on an embryo just a few days old. He was fascinated to see that surgery on limb buds influenced nerve growth in the spinal column. That fascination became his lifelong career. New findings came out of his laboratory through the 1980s, at which point he picked up the pen and wrote several important books on the history of embryology.

On June 14, 2001, Viktor Hamburger died. He was nearly 101 years old. For his longevity, his productivity, his important ideas, and his years of teaching, Hamburger has been called "one of the most influential scientists in neurobiology and development."*

* Comment by Dale Purves, Professor of Neuroscience, Duke University, quoted in Kathryn Brown, "A Lifelong Fascination with the Chick Embryo," *Science* 290 (2000): 1284.

membrane. When that happened, the whole cluster of cells would shrink and the nerve fiber they formed would retract. "The impression was that of a battlefield covered with corpses," she noted, but there were "cells able to ingest and destroy bacteria and the detritus [dead material] of other, degenerated cells," as if cell crews had been sent onto the battlefields to remove the corpses of their companions. "The scenarios I observed through the eyepieces impressed me not only because of their dramatic and dynamic character, but also, and even more, because they showed that the nervous system employed a strategy completely different from what had until then been attributed to it," she wrote later. While others had assumed that every developed cell stayed in its place for the long run, Levi-Montalcini recognized that cell growth happened in a variety of ways, including "active migration" and "drastic eliminations" of cells as a body grows. [56] In short, the organization of nerve cells into a nerve system included the death of old cells as well as the birth of new ones.

Viktor Hamburger agreed: it was an observation of great significance, worthy of publication. It took the two of them more than a year to replicate the findings. They chronicled normal chick embryo development as a baseline, focusing on the fifth through ninth day of growth, when cells multiply and differentiate most intensely. They refined an observation that Levi-Montalcini and Levi had made earlier, namely, that the cells in question can be divided into two types: large ones that grow and change very fast, and small ones that grow later and change more slowly. They decided to observe embryos with both reduced and enlarged peripheral areas. In other words, they removed wing or leg buds from some chick embryos, while transplanting a second wing or leg into others. Cells degenerated and disappeared in the spinal cords of embryos that lost limb buds, while more cells than normal grew in the spinal cords of those with extra limbs. Their findings indicated that "peripheral factors control the differentiation process," as they wrote in their summary. [57] Viktor Hamburger and Rita Levi-Montalcini's paper, "Proliferation, Differentiation and Degeneration in the Spinal Ganglia of the Chick Embryo under Normal and Experimental Conditions," appeared in the August 1949 issue of the *Journal of Experimental Zoology.*

INTRODUCING MOUSE TUMORS

Meanwhile Elmer Bueker, a scientist in New York who had studied with Viktor Hamburger, had been conducting a series of experiments that, at a glance, had little to do with the work going on in the Washington University laboratory. He had published an article in 1948 reporting that when he grafted bits of mouse tumor into chick embryos, nerve cells grew way beyond normal. Viktor Hamburger saw possible links between Bueker's findings and the work going on in their laboratory. He showed the paper to Rita Levi-Montalcini. "The effect Bueker described struck me like a message in cipher whose meaning it was up to us to discover," she wrote in her autobiography. [58] (For more information on Bueker's work, enter "Elmer Bueker" into a search engine and browse the sites listed.)

To begin with, she and Hamburger decided to repeat Bueker's experiments. They ordered specimens from an institute that specialized in breeding mice infected with the specific type of tumor that Bueker had used. Soon they received a box full of small albino mice, all carrying mouse sarcoma number 180. Even though some had tumors large enough to make their bodies bulge, the mice were lively and alert. It was Rita Levi-Montalcini's job to excise from these mice, as needed, bits of their tumors. She grafted those bits of tissue carefully into eggs containing three-day-old chicken embryos. A few days later, she used delicate tools to take sections out of those embryos, slicing the tissue she obtained as sliver-thin as possible, then mounting it on microscope slides and staining it with silver nitrate.

As she gazed through the microscope lens, she saw "an extraordinary spectacle."

> The mass of tumoral cells, which differed from those of the embryos in being larger and more intense yellow and in having a different growth pattern, were from all sides penetrated by bundles of brown-blackish nerve fibers. These fiber bundles passed between the cells like rivulets of water flowing steadily over a bed of stones. [59]

Something was making the chick embryo's nerve cells grow vigorously toward the tumor and form fibers that wrapped around the tumor's cells. Even the ganglia, or nerve masses, out of which the fibers grew seemed to have increased in size on the side where the tumor tissue was implanted.

This was an effect quite different from the one Levi-Montalcini had observed when she and Hamburger transplanted an extra wing or leg onto the embryo. She ran the mouse sarcoma 180 experiment again and again, coming up with the same results. "I had the feeling—a feeling that with the passing weeks became ever more certain," wrote Levi-Montalcini, "that I had come upon a phenomenon without precedent in the rich case history of experimental embryology." [60]

VERIFYING HER FINDINGS
Again, a bit of serendipity changed the course of science. A new delivery of tumor-treated mice arrived, but these carried not sarcoma 180 but sarcoma 37, a different tumor. Levi-Montalcini went ahead and used tumor tissue from those mice, too. The results she saw under her microscope were even more amazing than the last. A "thick network of nerve fibers"

invaded not only the tumor cells but also the primitive organs of the embryo. Levi-Montalcini could see "a chaotic and random distribution of fibers" in among the cells that were destined to become the kidney, the spleen, the thyroid, the liver, and the sexual organs. [61] The nerve cells even grew into developing blood vessels. What's more, all this growth happened long before a normal embryo would have developed nerves to serve those organs.

She kept repeating the experiment, so amazed by her results that she feared they would never happen again. And yet they did, over and over. She became more and more convinced that the tumor tissue released a fluid that had the power to accelerate nerve cell growth in the direction from which the fluid came. Whatever it was, this fluid factor in the mouse sarcoma was so strong, it could even make nerves grow in odd directions and to excessively large sizes. Levi-Montalcini felt the excitement building. She knew she was on to something important but, as she wrote four decades later, "the new field of research that was opening before my eyes was, in reality, much vaster than I could possibly have imagined." [62]

On one of these days, as Rita Levi-Montalcini was repeating with wonder the sarcoma 37 experiment, she heard a familiar voice thundering from out in the hallway. The "master," her former professor, Giuseppe Levi, had arrived without announcement at her Washington University lab. She eagerly told him of her current work and showed him what could be seen that day in the microscope. "Levi shook his powerful leonine head, still covered with a thick red mane in spite of his eighty-one years," she wrote later. [63]

"How can you say such nonsense?" he boomed. [64] *Those are not nerve fibers, they are connective fibers,* he insisted, and warned his former student not to continue down the path she was on. Connective tissue, such as bone and cartilage, provides support for other tissues and organs. Publishing such a mistaken analysis would ruin her reputation and his, he ranted.

Rita Levi-Montalcini remembered that in years past, such insults from Levi would have made her cringe with self-doubt, but now she had more self-confidence. She was certain of her findings. She just didn't want to spend all her energy arguing with her mentor.

> Suddenly, I had a good idea, and asked whether he had ever seen the Grand Canyon—a hypocritical question, as I knew perfectly well that this was his first trip to the United States (also, as it turned out, his last). In a few minutes, he had agreed to take immediate advantage of St. Louis's relative proximity to Arizona to see that stupendous panorama. Three days later, he flew back from Phoenix, in an excellent mood and completely covered with snow, then falling thick in St. Louis. [65]

With Levi happily dispatched elsewhere, Levi-Montalcini designed another experiment and determined definitively that the fibrous growth was not connective tissue.

Later that year, 1951, Rita Levi-Montalcini presented her laboratory findings at a symposium held at the New York Academy of Sciences. She titled her talk "The Chick Embryo in Biological Research," a signal that even she did not yet know what her most important finding was going to be. Despite its nondescript title, the talk caught the eye of science notables attending the symposium. One, neurophysiologist Paul Weiss, called Levi-Montalcini's "the most exciting discovery of the year." [66] He must have been judging with well-seasoned intuition, for it would be another three years before Levi-Montalcini's discovery was even given a name.

Nerve Growth Factor Gets a Name and a Reputation

1952–1959

6

TAKING MICE TO RIO

To learn more about the mystery factor that made nerve cells grow, Rita Levi-Montalcini needed to use a different investigative technique. Instead of removing sections of tissue from growing embryos, she needed to culture the cells of interest in vitro, in glass dishes, where she could isolate the cells she was studying from others in the growing body. She had learned that technique many years ago, in Giuseppe Levi's laboratory. Techniques had improved since then, but Hamburger's St. Louis lab was not equipped for such experiments. She needed to work with scientists expert in the new in vitro techniques. Luckily, she had a connection.

Hertha Meyer had been another student of Giuseppe Levi's at the University of Turin. She and Levi-Montalcini had kept in touch over the years. In 1939, Meyer had moved to Rio de Janeiro, Brazil, where she was now director of a tissue culture unit in the Biophysics Institute of the city's medical school. Her supervisor was Carlos Chagas, a neurophysiologist renowned for his work on how tropical fish generate electric current. His father, also named Carlos Chagas, had discovered trypanosomiasis, a severe South American parasitic infection now called Chagas' disease. (For more information on this disease, enter "Chagas' disease" into a search engine and browse the sites listed.)

When Meyer mentioned to Chagas that Rita Levi-Montalcini needed an in vitro culture lab to carry on her neuroscience, he invited her to Brazil. She arrived in Rio de Janeiro in September, smuggling in two fellow travelers: little white mice, blithe carriers of mouse sarcomas 180 and 37. Their keeper had found a little cardboard box, and in it they fit inside her overcoat pocket. She had poked several holes in the side of the box and tucked in thin slices of apple, enough to keep them fed and hydrated during the trip. From these two mice, Rita Levi-Montalcini planned to culture the tumor cells so critical to her experimental progress.

For the first months, Levi-Montalcini's experiments produced few significant results. She decided she should use not tumor cells from the mice directly but should first implant them into chick embryos, then extract bits of them for her in vitro experiments. Putting the tumor cells into the glass dish alongside nerve cells, she began to see dramatic results. "Nerve fibers had grown out in twelve hours from the entire periphery of sensory and sympathetic ganglia cultured in proximity to the [tumor] tissues and had spread out radially around the explants like the rays of the sun," she wrote years later. [67] She called the growth, a multitude of cell strands growing out in all directions from a common center, a "halo." With no camera to use, she picked up a pen and made drawings of the halo formations that she observed in the glass dishes.

Continuing to work for several more months in Rio, verifying and clarifying her experimental results, Rita Levi-Montalcini became "ever more convinced that the fibrillar halo, or halo of fibers," as she called it, "would provide us with the philosopher's stone for explaining the nature and action of the mysterious factor released by the tumors." [68] One advantage to the in vitro techniques was their speed. While her earlier experiments had taken weeks, while the embryos developed in their natural progression, nerve cells developed in vitro, when spurred on by the presence of the tumor in the same glass dish, in a matter of minutes and hours. Levi-Montalcini returned to St. Louis confident that she was on a new and promising research path.

COLLABORATING WITH COHEN

A new scientist had joined Viktor Hamburger's laboratory team at Washington University. Stanley Cohen had come to St. Louis as a postdoctoral fellow in physico-chemistry, the study of the physics of chemical components. He had recently earned a Ph.D. in biochemistry at the University of Michigan, where he wrote his dissertation on earthworm metabolism. Years later, Cohen recalled with some amusement the many nights he had spent roaming the university campus, collecting a total of 5,000 earthworms as his research subjects.

Viktor Hamburger had suggested that Stanley Cohen work with Rita Levi-Montalcini on the problems she was bringing back with her from Rio. The two began communicating daily, comparing notes, analyzing findings, and designing new experiments in which Cohen's chemistry background complemented the cellular observations Levi-Montalcini was collecting. Together, wrote Levi-Montalcini, "we witnessed with trepidation and disbelief the sequence of events, each turn of which revealed new properties of that mysterious character who, having made an appearance in Rio, received identification papers in 1954, to become known as Nerve Growth Factor, or NGF for short." [69]

In some ways, theirs was an unlikely partnership. She was a neuroembryologist, he was a biochemist. She had grown up in the ancient city of Turin, while he had grown up in fast-paced New York. "I have often asked myself what lucky star caused our paths to cross," [70] Levi-Montalcini wrote in 1988. Her memories of Cohen in the early 1950s, when they worked together in St. Louis, show the warm affection that she held for him.

> He would arrive in the morning with a pipe in his mouth, limping slightly because he had had polio as a child, after traveling the short distance that separated his prefabricated cottage . . . from Rebstock Hall, where our institute was. He was followed by Smog, the sweetest and most mongrel dog I ever saw. Smog used to lie down at Stan's feet when he sat at his desk, and kept a loving eye on him, or slept when he fidgeted with test tubes or relaxed playing the flute. [71]

Cohen's feelings were equally positive toward her. "Rita," she remembers his saying one day, "you and I are good, but together we are wonderful." [72] They worked together at Washington University for only six years, but Levi-Montalcini remembers those as "the six most intense and productive years of my life." [73]

Cohen approached the mystery factor as a biochemist, eager to discover its chemical and molecular properties. To do so, however, he had to find ways to isolate the critical growth-inducing component from the tumor in which Bueker and Levi-Montalcini had found it. Through months of testing, he found that it was a nucleoprotein, in Levi-Montalcini's words, "a macromolecule formed by complexes of nucleic acids and proteins." [74] That was a start, but it wasn't the final answer. Cohen needed to identify the components of that macromolecule further.

Once again chance stepped in, although Rita Levi-Montalcini wouldn't see it that way. "In a biological science," she writes,

> perhaps to a larger extent than in any other experimental science, chance and good luck play a notoriously great role. It is not only, as is so often stated, a matter of serendipity, or of the perception of a truth that is there all the time but goes unnoticed until the mind of the observer suddenly grasps it, but rather of a fortuitous stumbling into a cave of precious stones while hiking up a hill on a trail that is not expected to bring one anywhere but to the top of the hill. [75]

Whether chance, wisdom, or "fortuitous stumbling," Stanley Cohen took the advice of Arthur Kornberg, a fellow biochemist who told him that snake venom contained an enzyme that could eat away the nucleic acids in the macromolecule. Use the resulting chemical in your experiments, suggested Kornberg. If it works the same as always, you know that the proteins are the active components. If not, you know that the nucleic acids are.

What did happen was something that no one expected. When the snake venom was added into the experiment, the halo produced was outlandishly denser in fibers than anyone in the laboratory had seen before. What had happened? "Two alternatives were considered," explained Levi-Montalcini. Either there was something in the tumor that inhibited this extreme halo response and the venom had killed it, or the venom added even more growth factor. "Six hours later we knew the answer," Levi-Montalcini wrote. [76] Into a culture dish prepared with nerve ganglia, they introduced snake venom only. A dense halo developed immediately. Snake venom contained the mystery factor that spurred nerve growth, too.

MEETING THE MYSTERY FACE TO FACE

Cohen and Levi-Montalcini busily proceeded on their parallel research paths. He worked to purify and characterize the growth-spurring factor, a thousand times more concentrated in snake venom than in mouse sarcoma and thus easier to isolate. She proceeded with in vitro experiments similar to those she had conducted in Rio, but this time she introduced snake venom, not mouse tumor, into the cultures. She found that its biological activity was similar, if not identical, to that of the tumors. Putting their findings together, they proposed the existence of an organic chemical, found in a variety of living things, which moves as a fluid through growing tissue, stimulating and influencing cells in the developing nervous system. In a landmark paper published by Cohen, Levi-Montalcini, and Hamburger in 1954, they proposed that this mystery fluid be called Nerve Growth Factor. It quickly became known as NGF.

If NGF existed as these researchers proposed, then it should exist elsewhere in the world of living things. Levi-Montalcini and Cohen prepared an extract from the saliva glands of healthy mice, the equivalent of one tiny gland in 50 liters of saline solution. They introduced it into the glass dish with nerve cells. "The following morning we marveled, with a mixture of happiness and incredulity, at results far surpassing our greatest expectations," recalled Levi-Montalcini. "Fibrillar halos had grown around the ganglia." [77]

This finding brought the research to three basic questions: What was the nature of this very potent salivary NGF? What were its actions on nerve cells, both as they developed and after they had differentiated? Why did mouse glands produce NGF? Stanley Cohen tackled the first question. Rita Levi-Montalcini took on the second. The third question, they agreed, they would have to put aside, "resigning ourselves to accepting the NGF molecule as one of the many offerings that Nature makes without explaining their meaning." [78] As Levi-Montalcini points out in her autobiography, this decision was a wise one. It would take another quarter-century before she and other researchers found the answer to the third question.

A MEMORABLE EVENT IN NEUROEMBRYOLOGY

In the neuroembryology laboratories of Washington University, the next few months were frantic with the spirit of discovery. Stanley Cohen succeeded in characterizing the active ingredient in salivary NGF as a protein molecule similar to that of snake venom NGF. Rita Levi-Montalcini injected salivary NGF daily into newborn rodents, then observed the effects on a cellular level. Sympathetic nerve ganglia increased in size in just a few days' time. Nerves multiplied, connecting to internal organs and to the skin, distinctly so in newborns and even noticeably so in adults. The pace of work, collaboration, mutual analysis, and shared success was invigorating, so it came as a shock when Viktor Hamburger announced that he had not been given enough funding to hire Stanley Cohen as a permanent faculty member. "I saw coming to an end the most productive period of my life," Rita Levi-Montalcini wrote in her autobiography, "and also the most picturesque in the saga of NGF, when Stan with his magical intuition and flute played the part of the wizard, charming snakes at will and getting the miraculous fluid to flow forth from the minuscule mouths of mice." [79]

Before he left St. Louis, though, Stanley Cohen and Rita Levi-Montalcini conducted one more essential experiment in the process toward confirming the presence and function of Nerve Growth Factor: they tested the reverse of its activity. Cohen had already observed that snake venom antiserum could slow down nerve growth. He concocted an antiserum specific to salivary NGF and introduced it in experiments parallel to those they had conducted before. It did inhibit nerve growth. Levi-Montalcini even injected it into newborn rats, then operated on them a few days later to discover that, miraculously, the size of some nerve-growth areas had decreased, while others had developed as they would under normal conditions. While Cohen and Levi-Montalcini found those results interesting, their mentor, Viktor Hamburger, found them momentous. He knew that this discovery would lead to an even clearer understanding of NGF. "Remember the date of this finding," he told them; it was June 11, 1959. "It marks a memorable event in neuroembryology." [80] Years later, Rita Levi-Montalcini would look back on that date as the starting point of her deeper understanding of the Nerve Growth Factor, a discovery and understanding for which she and Stanley Cohen would, 27 years later, be awarded the Nobel Prize.

One month later, Cohen left St. Louis, headed for Vanderbilt University in Nashville, Tennessee. As Rita Levi-Montalcini proceeded to learn more about Nerve Growth Factor, Stanley Cohen studied a parallel phenomenon, which he called Epidermal Growth Factor (EGF). Another protein molecule like NGF, EGF stimulates the growth of connective tissue, which supports and connects all other tissue in the body.

It was a bittersweet parting between Levi-Montalcini and Cohen. They would keep in touch, no doubt, and share their

Stanley Cohen and EGF

In 1959, Stanley Cohen left Washington University and the company of Rita Levi-Montalcini and Viktor Hamburger in the laboratory. He joined the biochemistry department of Vanderbilt University in Nashville, Tennessee, that same year. While Levi-Montalcini spent years refining her understanding of Nerve Growth Factor (NGF), Cohen concentrated on another component he found when analyzing the chemistry of nervous system development.

He had noticed that when he injected salivary gland extract into newborn mice, it caused certain things to happen sooner than normal. An injected mouse opened its eyes at least a week sooner than its littermates. Its teeth matured faster, too, pushing through the gum several days earlier than normal. Apparently there was another growth factor, different from NGF, contained in the salivary gland extract. Thus began Stanley Cohen's research on the substance he named Epidermal Growth Factor, or EGF, because it encouraged growth on the outer surface, or epidermis, of the body.

In a number of ways, Cohen's work paralleled Levi-Montalcini's. He and colleagues purified EGF and then determined the amino acid sequence in its molecular structure. Researchers have shown that EGF stimulates cell growth in many organs of the body, and those findings carry important implications for its use in both the study and the cure of cancer. As studies inspired by Cohen's work on EGF brought a clearer understanding of how cells grow normally, those findings were carried over and used in laboratory experiments to observe how cells, including cancer cells, grow abnormally. Knowledge about EGF led to the discovery of oncogenes, special genes that play an important part in transforming normal cells into cancerous ones.

ideas for years to come. But that was not the same as meeting in offices and working side by side in laboratories, discussing their observations, brainstorming together, several times a day. They must have said goodbye in their understated ways, and then, Rita Levi-Montalcini remembered in her autobiography, "he set out with his limping step, smoking his pipe, Smog as always at his side. I followed them from the window while thinking back with gratitude on the years spent together and looking forward with anxiety to those I would have to face without his precious aid." [81]

NGF Comes of Age:
Investigations
Around the World

1960–1985

The Electron Microscope

In the 1930s, when Rita Levi-Montalcini first began her scientific investigations, only light microscopes were in use. A mirror or light source shot light up through the prepared slide. The investigator looked through eyepieces and down a configuration of lenses that magnified the illuminated object under study. Samples too thick simply blocked the light, which is one reason why it was so important for investigators to prepare extremely thin slices of tissue.

Light microscopes had a limit to the magnification they could provide. As scientists wanted to view things even smaller, like cells and their component parts, they needed instruments that could magnify further. Electron microscopes filled that need.

First developed in Germany in the early 1930s, electron microscopes did not become common in laboratories until the 1960s. Instead of using light to view an object, electron microscopes use electrons, negatively charged components of an atom, which can be focused much more finely than light. The specimen to be viewed is placed inside a vacuum-sealed chamber. The instrument fires a beam of electrons at the specimen. Some electrons bounce off and some travel through. One type, the scanning electron microscope (SEM), records the patterns made by the electrons that bounce off. Another, the transmission electron microscope (TEM), records the patterns of electrons that travel through. The two types serve different purposes, depending on the sort of specimen to be observed.

Scanning electron microscopes can magnify specimens more than 100 million times their original size. This means that with them, researchers can observe things as small as 10 nanometers, or 1/10,000,000 of a meter. Some of the newest technologies can view things even smaller. Electron microscopes allow scientists today to view cells and their contents, viruses, bacteria, molecules, and even atoms.

heart of her work all along. She remembered the days when she and Viktor Hamburger thought they were on to something— when they saw how mouse tumor cells made chick embryo nerve cells grow—but they didn't even have a name for what caused it. She could practically feel that Rio sun that shone down on her on the day she saw for the first time, with pride and amazement, how a halo of neurofibrils was growing in her little glass dishes. She thought back warmly on the months Stanley Cohen and she worked together, and how together they wrote the landmark articles that announced their identification of a Nerve Growth Factor. And now, in the 1970s, across the United States, in Australia, Italy, and elsewhere, scientists were working hard to learn more about the still-elusive NGF. "Now that the NGF has come of age and the most picturesque and adventurous phase of its life is over," she wrote to conclude the chapter, "the biographer, who has had some part in the chase, entrusts it, with love, to younger and more skillful hands." [89]

TWO SAD GOODBYES IN TWO YEARS' TIME

At the time that she wrote her apparent farewell to NGF, Rita Levi-Montalcini was 64 years old, one year short of the age traditionally considered appropriate for retirement. It had been 30 years since she had arrived in Viktor Hamburger's laboratory in St. Louis, expecting to stay about a year. For all those years, she had spent one month each summer back in Italy, visiting her family. But as she aged, she more strongly felt the pull of family ties. The new center in Rome had given her reason to travel to Italy more often, but when she was there, her focus was still on work, not on family.

All of her family still lived in Turin. Her brother and older sister had families of their own. Like herself, her twin sister, Paola, had never married. Indeed, their lives had followed similar patterns, even though they had seen little of each other for three decades. Paola Levi-Montalcini had worked intensely under the mentorship of a great master, the Italian artist Felice Casorati, very much her version of Rita's relationship with Giuseppe Levi. By 1960, Paola Levi-Montalcini had earned recognition and respect as an important Italian painter, engraver, and sculptor.

In 1963, Adele Levi-Montalcini, Rita and Paola's mother, had taken a fall and fractured her thighbone. For a woman of her age, that sort of injury can be serious. Rita, spending some time at her laboratory in Rome, was able to be with her during her convalescence. A second operation left her pale with pain, feverish, and asthmatic. All four of her children took their turns at her bedside. When her condition improved, Rita left Turin to return to the lab in Rome. "A new researcher had just joined our group," she wrote 25 years later, "and I felt it my duty to see that she was 'broken in.' Was it really a good enough reason for me to leave Mother, even if only for a couple of days?" [90] That question was to haunt her for years to come, she wrote, because, the very day after she departed, she received a call from Paola, urging her to come back to Turin. Their mother would soon die.

Rita Levi-Montalcini sat at the bedside, looking at her mother, still breathing yet not to come back to consciousness ever again. "I held her deathly pale hand in my own," wrote Levi-Montalcini, and

> kept repeating to myself that nothing could ever, until the end of my own life, alter the ties that had bound us since my birth. She herself, when I left Italy each year after my brief summer stays, encouraged me to face our separations serenely, in the same way as I would some day courageously have to confront our definitive parting. . . . That day had come; and though I tried to find comfort in the thought that death had come stealthily and been sweet for her, I felt as if the thread of my own life had also been cut. [91]

Less than two years later, Rita Levi-Montalcini faced the death of another person dear to her: Giuseppe Levi. Hearing that her mentor had been hospitalized in late January 1965, she went to visit him in the hospital in Turin. He had just turned 92. In the same voice that used to thunder down the halls of the Institute of Anatomy, Levi greeted her, saying "I have a carcinoma of the stomach . . . I diagnosed it myself . . . I'll die in two weeks. I don't regret it. On the contrary, I'm happy for it. I've already lived too long." [92]

Then he demanded, "Tell me about your work." Levi-Montalcini spoke with a combination of pride and sadness about the promising results she and her colleagues in the United States and Italy were experiencing. They talked for three hours, Levi holding his protegee's hand tightly. "We reminisced about what we had enjoyed and suffered together in the past," she later recalled, "about my anguish at not having been able to unravel the mechanisms behind the cerebral convolutions in the brain of human fetuses. He smiled, recalling those times, and squeezed my hand to show he had forgiven me my youthful ineptitude." [93] Giuseppe Levi died, as he had predicted, two weeks later.

UNWINDING THE HUMAN NERVE GROWTH FACTOR

By the time of her mother and Levi's deaths, Rita Levi-Montalcini was spending almost as much time in Italy as she was in St. Louis. Her laboratory had received funding from the Consiglio Nazionale delle Ricerche, Italy's National Research Council, and the director of the biochemistry department at the Istituto Superiore di Sanitá had generously renovated building space to provide three large laboratory rooms with suitable instruments and equipment. "Within three months I had at my disposal a research unit larger than the one in the department of biology at Washington University," wrote Levi-Montalcini. "Thus I began my life as a commuter between two continents." [94] By 1969, the lab in Rome had grown to include projects in cell biology, genetics, and immunology and had taken on a new name: the Laboratory of Cell Biology. Since both of them were committed to work in the two laboratories, she and Pietro Angeletti agreed to alternate directorships between the laboratory groups in St. Louis and Rome.

It must have been gratifying for Rita Levi-Montalcini, through the 1970s, to recognize how many scientists from around the world were working on questions related to Nerve Growth Factor. She herself continued to work actively as well, collaborating often with two younger Italian scientists, Pietro Calissano and Luigi Aloe, whose names appear with hers at the head of numerous scholarly articles. In 1979, at the age of 70, Rita Levi-Montalcini formally resigned as director of the Laboratory of Cell Biology, but she continued to be "allowed," to use her humble language, "to continue to work in the capacity of a guest in the institute." [95] Support from the Italian government had dropped significantly in the years since the laboratory's founding, yet in the world's science community, enthusiasm for the work going on there had skyrocketed.

For one thing, research techniques had advanced. Once James Watson and Francis Crick took their pioneering steps in the early 1960s, which led to an understanding of the structure and function of DNA, the molecule that encodes genetic information, new ways of looking at molecules and a new curiosity about how they worked swept the field of biochemistry. In 1984, Levi-Montalcini and colleagues published an overview of work on NGF. "After three decades of studies since its discovery," they summarized, "NGF is finding its proper place in developmental neurobiology, and its important functional role would suggest the existence of a family of similar molecules acting upon other neuronal target cells. From fish and amphibians up to mammals, the action of NGF . . . seems to be a crucial one." [96]

By the 1980s, investigators were using new technologies and genetic engineering techniques to explore nerve cells and the role played by NGF in their normal functioning. Their discoveries hinted at ways that knowledge about NGF could play a part in the treatment of diseases of the nervous system. A momentous stride forward occurred in 1983, when a research team announced that they had located the NGF gene on the short arm of chromosome number one in the human genome. Such a location suggested that NGF was situated in a vulnerable place, a chromosomal region that could be more easily damaged or deleted than others. This finding was full of implications for NGF's role in diseases of the nervous system. Once the genetic code for human NGF had been mapped out, laboratories were able to follow it precisely and produce pure synthetic NGF, which opened up possibilities for its use in medicine. Medical researchers moved forward on that front, investigating what effects the deletion of the NGF gene could have on a developing human being and, on the other hand, whether NGF could be a cure for disease.

Surveying the work going on around the world, all stemming from her original discoveries about the Nerve Growth Factor, Rita Levi-Montalcini used her autobiography to voice the hope that motivated many to keep exploring the amazing chemical:

> Will the NGF derived from this new source [the human chromosome]—and now no longer collected from neoplastic [tumor] tissues (whose reasons for producing it, by the way, are still cloaked in mystery) or from the mouths of snakes and mice, but, aseptically distilled in the laboratory—be able to bring back order to the functionally impaired neuronal circuitries of that immensely complex entity, the brain of *Homo sapiens?*[97]

It was this sense of promise, and this certainty of the significance of her pioneering work, that brought Rita Levi-Montalcini to the top of the list of candidates for the Nobel Prize in Medicine in the year 1986.

The Nobel Prize
and Beyond

1986–

8

ACCEPTING THE PRIZE ON BEHALF OF NGF

From the key moments of discovery in Rio de Janeiro, Rita Levi-Montalcini often associated the colorful but concealing carnival masks of that Brazilian city with the mysteriousness of her lifelong object of study. "It was in the anticipatory, pre-Carnival atmosphere of Rio de Janeiro that in 1952 NGF lifted its mask to reveal its miraculous ability to cause the growth, in the space of a few hours, of dense auras of nervous fibers," she wrote in her autobiography. [98]

In her own description of the momentous evening in Stockholm, Sweden, in December 1986, when she received the Nobel Prize, Levi-Montalcini playfully extended the metaphor, turning NGF into a masked mystery guest and leaving herself out of the limelight.

> NGF appeared in public under large floodlights, amid the splendor of a vast hall adorned for celebration, in the presence of the royals of Sweden, of princes, of ladies in rich and gala dresses, and gentlemen in tuxedos. Wrapped in a black mantle, he bowed before the king and, for a moment, lowered the veil covering his face. We recognized each other in a matter of seconds when I saw him looking for me among the applauding crowd. He then replaced his veil and disappeared as suddenly as he had appeared. Has he gone back to an errant life in the forests inhabited by the spirits who drift at night along the frozen lakes of the North, where I spent so many solitary, enchanted hours of my youth? Will we see each other again? Or was that instant the fulfillment of my desire of many years to meet him, and I have henceforth lost trace of him forever? [99]

Of course, for those in attendance, the figures appearing in the spotlight were Stanley Cohen and Rita Levi-Montalcini, who shared the honor of receiving the 1986 Nobel Prize in Medicine.

The History of the Nobel Prize

Alfred Bernhard Nobel was born in Sweden in 1833 but spent much of his youth in St. Petersburg, Russia, where his father taught him the family trade: manufacturing explosives. Working in the family business outside Stockholm, he helped develop a chemical combination of nitroglycerine and gunpowder, used to blast out earth for building roads, canals, and tunnels. But the explosive was unpredictable and hard to handle, and Alfred Nobel felt ashamed when his family's product killed innocent workers. He was determined to design a safer explosive. The result: dynamite.

His invention made him millions. When he died, in 1896, his family members were shocked to learn that he had left all his fortune to establish a foundation that would award prizes to those individuals, from anywhere in the world, whose work had made the greatest contributions to human progress in that year. He designated that prizes should be awarded in five areas: peace, literature, physics, chemistry, and medicine or physiology. In 1968 a sixth Nobel Prize category was added: economics.

Nobel Prize winners receive a medal and a money award whose value varies with the economic climate, since it con-sists of the interest drawn that year from the original Nobel investment. Today, the dollar value of the prize is about one million dollars.

The first winner of the Nobel Prize for Medicine or Physiology, the same prize that Rita Levi-Montalcini won, was Emil von Behring, a German doctor and professor of hygiene whose discoveries led to immunizations against diphtheria and tubercu-losis. In 2003, Paul Lauterbur of Urbana, Illinois, and Sir Peter Mansfield of Nottingham, United Kingdom, shared the prize for their work on magnetic resonance imaging. For more information on the Nobel Prize and its history, visit the Nobel e-Museum at http://www.nobel.se/index.html.

Introducing the award recipients was Professor Kerstin Hall, an endocrinologist from the Karolinska Hospital in Stockholm. "We have all been small infants who have grown tall," he began his presentation speech. Growth from birth on is regulated by hormones released from the pituitary gland, but what of growth before birth? he asked, setting up the context in which to explain the importance of Cohen and Levi-Montalcini's work.

> The pattern of growth and differentiation has long been established, but the mechanisms regulating prenatal development remained unknown—growth hormone does not control these events. The discovery of growth factors in tissues other than the pituitary led to a new understanding—growth and differentiation are regulated by signal substances released from cells and acting on neighbouring cells. The first such signal substances to be identified were Nerve Growth Factor (NGF) and Epidermal Growth Factor (EGF). The discovery of NGF by Rita Levi-Montalcini and EGF by Stanley Cohen initiated a new era in the research area of growth and differentiation and was followed by the identification of several other growth factors released by different types of cells. [100]

"The discovery, identification and isolation of NGF created a breakthrough in the research field of developmental neurobiology," continued Hall. "For the first time a chemically well-characterized substance became available for use in studies of nerve growth." [101] NGF held great promise in the treatment of central nervous system diseases, as Cohen's EGF had been found to help heal wounds in the eye's cornea, the skin, and the intestines, and to help in the treatment of burns. [102]

"Stanley Cohen is the brilliant biochemist who purified the first growth factors and improved our understanding about how a growth signal from the outside is relayed into the cells," concluded Professor Hall. "Rita Levi-Montalcini is the great developmental biologist who showed how the outgrowth of the nerves was regulated." He invited the two laboratory partners and old friends to step forward and receive their Nobel Prize "from the hands of His Majesty the King," Carl Gustaf XVI of Sweden. [103]

The press release broadcast by the Nobel Assembly to announce their decision explained in similar language why Levi-Montalcini and Cohen received the prize. Their work contributed both to basic science and to the future of medicine.

> The discovery of NGF and EGF has opened new fields of widespread importance to basic science. As a direct consequence we may increase our understanding of many disease states such as developmental malformations, degenerative changes in senile dementia, delayed wound healing and tumour diseases. The characterization of these growth factors is therefore expected, in the near future, to result in the development of new therapeutic agents and improved treatment in various clinical diseases. [104]

The press release listed several other growth factors discovered and isolated during the 1980s: somatomedin, an insulin-like substance that affects growth; platelet-derived growth factor (PDGF), which stimulates the growth of cells in blood vessels, connective tissue, and lymphatic tissue; and interleukin-2, which stimulates blood cell growth in the immune system and is being studied for the treatment of cancer and AIDS. "All research groups who discovered 'new' growth factors have followed in the tracks of Levi-Montalcini and Cohen," announced the Nobel committee. "In the research area of growth factors and their biological action, Levi-Montalcini and Cohen have created a scientific school with an increasing number of followers." [105]

It is expected that recipients of the Nobel Prize will present two speeches: one lecture, explaining the work for which they are being honored; and one acceptance speech, shorter and more personal, at the awards banquet (Appendix A). In her lecture, Rita Levi-Montalcini emphasized how important it was for people to understand that during the 1940s, when she began her work, interest in experimental neurobiology was waning. This was an atmosphere, she explained, in which "an unforeseeable turn of events . . . resulted in the discovery of the Nerve Growth Factor." [106] She proceeded to summarize the key events in the history of NGF research, characteristically downplaying her own part in the process by elevating the visibility of other researchers and of the central character, NGF itself. She returned several times to the theme of the surprise factor in her career, using the NGF example to encourage other scientists to venture on beyond the realms of the known, the obvious, the acceptable, and the predictable.

> Predictions of the unpredictable are encouraged by the same history of NGF, which may be defined as a long sequence of unanticipated events which each time resulted in a new turn in the NGF uncharted route, and opened new vistas on an ever-changing panorama. This trend, which became manifest from the very beginning and in fact alerted me to the existence of NGF, is perhaps the most attractive, even though elusive, trait of this 35-year-long adventure. One can at present only predict where future developments are most likely to occur. [107]

While Levi-Montalcini emphasized NGF's elusiveness, Stanley Cohen emphasized the relative isolation from the scientific community in which the two of them worked early on. When a reporter from *Science* magazine interviewed him, preparing to write an article about the prizes he and Levi-Montalcini had just won, he explained to her that in the early years, many scientists were skeptical of the direction they were taking in their work. "This had the advantage that people left you alone and you weren't competing with the world," Cohen said. "The disadvantage was that you had to convince people that what you were working with was real." As the reporter wrote to conclude her story, "It is safe to say that people are now convinced." [108]

BEYOND NGF

Since the time of her winning the Nobel Prize, Rita Levi-Montalcini has allowed her intellect to move beyond the field viewed through her microscope and into the hazier realms of the human character. She hinted at those ideas in the conclusion of her autobiography, *In Praise of Imperfection*, published in 1988. She titled her last chapter "Disharmony in a Complex System," and in it she returned to that research problem onto which dear Professor Levi had set her so many years before: the convolutions of the human brain. But now, instead of answering these questions through cellular observations, Levi-Montalcini reached out to evolutionary theory, history, philosophy, and her own life memories.

"What mysterious sequence of mutations caused the brain of our distant predecessors so to increase in volume, and its cortical mantle to expand, as if by levitation, and fold back upon itself in ever-more creases, or circumvolutions, as to fit within the limits set by the cranial capacity, unvaried over hundreds of thousands of years?" she asked. [109] And why is it that, with such multiple folds increasing the volume and activity within the human brain, we have developed in some areas on a path of unarguable progress, but in other areas seem not to have progressed at all? Language aided our forebears on the path of evolution, then writing ushered in a new phase of cultural evolution, newly present as a force in the continuing evolution of the human brain. Differential calculus, a product of the human symbol-making capability, led to the industrial and techno-logical revolutions of recent centuries.

Human evolution prepared the way for cultural evolution, wrote Levi-Montalcini. But those same evolutionary processes did not have the same progressive impact on "the limbic system, which governs the processing and expression of emotive and affective activities." [110] In simple language, the brain's ability to think, invent, and calculate has evolved further than its capacity to feel for others. That imbalance means that human history to the present day has included horrify-ing eras and episodes of violence, war, and genocide, as Levi-Montalcini bitterly remembered from her own youth. It cannot be argued, she insisted, that war and violence were inborn human traits. Unlike animals, humans continue to learn from surrounding adults, culture, and history throughout their lives, and human beings learn violence against one another, generation after generation. "The ethicosocial systems that individuals are exposed to while young," she explained, "condition their adult behavior as well, engendering tight bonds between members of the same ethnic group, who are united by a credo and ready to sacrifice everything in order to defend blindly accepted values." As an example, she raised the image of "the interminable ranks of the Hitler Youth," young men and women, who energetically supported anti-Semitism in Germany during World War II. [111] It was a sorrowful truth, connecting to painful memories in her own childhood.

Since the publication of her autobiography in 1988, Rita Levi-Montalcini has written eight more books. All were written in Italian; most have been translated into French, sometimes German, but not one has been translated into English, so Rita Levi-Montalcini's world view has not been available to American youth. One of the first books she chose to write during these later years of her life was titled *Il tuo futuro (Your Future)*, and in it she spoke directly to teenagers and young adults about the choices they had before them. She counseled youth to choose a life path both productive and ethical. In *La galassia mente* (*The Mind's Galaxy*), she expands upon her evolutionary meditation that ended her autobiography, sharing in more detail her understanding of the progressive changes in the capabilities of the human mind.

She dedicated *Un universo inquieto* (*A Restless Universe*) to the life and artistic accomplishments of her sister, Paola, who had become well known in her native country as an innovative painter and sculptor. Neither one of the twins had husbands or children, so when Rita returned to Italy in the early 1960s, needing a place to live during the periods when she worked at the Laboratory of Cell Biology, they began sharing an apartment on the Via di Villa Massimo in Rome. That was where both sisters were living when, in September 2000, Paola died. Soon thereafter, according to her sister's will, Rita Levi-Montalcini donated 44 of Paola Levi-Montalcini's paintings to the National Gallery of Modern Art in Rome.

In her most recent book, *Tempo di mutamenti* (*Time of Changes*), published in 2002, Rita Levi-Montalcini once again explores the possibility that the human race might evolve toward peace and kindness rather than violence and mutual destruction, a theme that has haunted her ever since she turned her study from science to philosophy. As cover art for this book, Rita Levi-Montalcini chose to use the painting for which Paola Levi-Montalcini is most famous, the Cubist-inspired *A Walking City,* painted in 1944 when the family was in hiding in Florence. In the painting, Rita Levi-Montalcini once wrote, she saw "a confused intertwining of human figures, represented . . . as broken vertical lines, crossed arms and bent heads, a chaotic complex of people and household effects which moved without fixed destination from one part of the city to the other." [112] It symbolized the counter forces at work in the world around her, a confused intertwining of hope and despair, acts of charity undone by acts of greed and hatred, and efforts toward peace contradicted by the drive to kill and conquer.

TO EASE THE PAIN OF THE WORLD

Approaching the last years of her life, Rita Levi-Montalcini noticed the stark contrast between the progress of her science and the progress of the world in which she lived. Journalists had called her discovery of NGF an example of concept coming out of chaos, and indeed there was a life-affirming orderliness to what had happened. She felt an intuition that something was there to be discovered. She sought it, whatever it was, diligently following the scientific method for years. Gradually she brought into view something that had been there all along yet had never before been noticed. In subsequent years, the concept that started as just a hunch became a known reality, a foundational concept in science and medicine, as numbers of other investigators joined the effort to characterize and understand Nerve Growth Factor.

But human civilization did not seem to be moving along the same slow but steady path toward progress and understanding. After coming to adulthood during a period in world history fraught with extreme hatred, fear, and violence, Rita Levi-Montalcini had reason to believe that life would get better. She watched such developments as the Cold War, a missile crisis, nuclear stand-offs, earth-threatening pollution, wars, terrorist attacks, and genocidal massacres in the Far East, the Middle East, Africa, Europe, and the Americas. Human beings did not seem able to progress up the same steady incline that science did.

She had never been an outspoken feminist, but in these years of reflection, Rita Levi-Montalcini quietly recognized how lucky she had been compared with most of womankind. In 1993, invited because of her continuing messages for world peace and equity among all individuals and races, she participated in a meeting of the International Council of Human Duties in Trieste, Italy. "During this meeting I stressed the fact that the art of war had been invented and managed exclusively by men," said Levi-Montalcini, "and expressed the hope that

Eve's descendants would have the far more arduous, but constructive, task of inventing and managing peace." [113]

Together with Roman sociologist Eleonora Barbiere Masini, Levi-Montalcini proposed that the organization create a network to help women living in dangerous areas or threatening situations. In 1995, they helped form the Women's International Network for Emergency and Solidarity (WIN). Soon thereafter, thanks to support from the European Union and the United Nations Educational, Scientific and Cultural Organization (UNESCO), the organization published a Directory of Women's Groups in Emergency Situations, which provides contact information for dozens of organizations dedicated to solving the problems faced by women around the world, from debt to drugs, from disease to forced prostitution. (For more information on the women's "International Network for Emergency and Solidarity," please enter this phrase into a search engine and browse the sites listed.)

"In every country social and cultural disparity has privileged members of the male gender," wrote Levi-Montalcini in her foreword to the WIN directory. "This is the primary cause of women's exclusion from positions of management at every level of human activity." A recent international Report on Human Development, she wrote, found that "only 6% of offices in the political and economic field are occupied by women." Citing work done by sociologist Masini, she observed that women's lives have always forced them to develop adaptability and flexibility. Those very qualities, said Levi-Montalcini, are the ones most essential for a world progressing toward peace, tolerance, and equity. "The problem is not so much, or not only, to give women a sense of dignity as thinking beings who are responsible for their actions, intellectually and morally," Levi-Montalcini concluded, "as to at last utilise a precious resource of intellectual energy, that has been ignored for millennia." [114]

Certainly she was not speaking of herself. Rita Levi-Montalcini is the exception that proves the rule. Born a woman in a man's world, born a Jew in a period of horrifying anti-Semitism, she had risen to levels of accomplishment few people, women or men, ever know. She had persisted in a field considered not promising, endured in work settings less than hospitable, and still she had achieved the peak of scientific success. She had trusted her own hunches and observations when others debunked them. In her own life story, she proved the "precious resource of intellectual energy" that can come bundled into a single determined woman. As she approached her 90s, Rita Levi-Montalcini sought ways to draw from all she had learned and give back to others.

"I have tried," she wrote in the introduction of her autobiography, "to reconcile two aspirations that the Irish poet William Butler Yeats deemed to be irreconcilable: perfection of the life and perfection of the work. By so doing, and in accordance with his predictions, I have achieved what might be termed 'imperfection of the life and of the work.'" In her characteristic way, she downplayed her own character and achievements. "The fact that the activities that I have carried out in such imperfect ways have been and still are for me a source of inexhaustible joy, leads me to believe that imperfection, rather than perfection, . . . is more in keeping with human nature." [115] At the same time, she expressed her love and tolerance for all humankind. If all were to seek the sort of imperfect life and work that Rita Levi-Montalcini has enjoyed, our world would be the better place that she envisions.

Appendices

Rita Levi-Montalcini's Acceptance Speech at the Nobel Banquet, December 10, 1986

Your Majesties, Your Royal Highnesses, Ladies and Gentlemen, It is with very deep emotion that my dear friend Stanley Cohen and I stand here today, in front of you, and wish to express our immense gratitude for having been bestowed with the greatest honor that a scientist can ever dream of receiving for his or her accomplishments: the Nobel Prize.

Stanley and I first began to work together thirty-three years ago in the Department of Zoology of the Washington University in St. Louis, Missouri, chaired at that time by Prof. Viktor Hamburger, a leading scientist in Experimental Neuroembryology, a great scholar and a most beloved master and friend. Since then, we enjoyed every minute of this adventure which was to lead us to Stockholm.

Stanley's exceptional talent and most rigorous training in biochemistry, and my own training in neurology, which I had the privilege of receiving from the famous Italian scientist, the late Giuseppe Levi, at the Medical School of the University of Turin, provided us with an ideal complementary background to tackle what at first seemed a fairly easy puzzle to solve: namely, to uncover the nature and mechanism of action of a protein molecule which became known, on account of its biological properties, as the "Nerve Growth Factor." It took, however, more than three decades to realize the complexity of the problem which is at present still under intensive investigation all over the world.

I wish to add that while Stanley devoted from 1961 to the present day all his skill and expertise in exploring another growth factor, the Epidermal Growth Factor, in the Department of Biochemistry of the University in Nashville, Tennessee, I was most fortunate to be joined twenty years ago by Prof. Pietro Calissano and Luigi Aloe, two outstanding investigators and dearest friends, who worked daily with me or independently, and to whom goes most of the merit for the success in our recent studies of the Nerve Growth Factor.

As far as I am concerned, I must add that the Nerve Growth Factor would perhaps never have been discovered were it not for the rigorous neurobiological training which I received in my native country, at the University of Turin, and of the most generous hospitality and invaluable scientific and technical help which I received at Washington University, where I spent the thirty happiest and most productive years of my life.

To our Swedish colleagues and dear friends, I wish to express my everlasting gratitude for their fundamental contributions in the field of Neurosciences. To them we all are indebted for having opened the gates of the golden era in the field of neurobiology, and I personally feel, even more than anybody else, thankful for their outstanding work in the area of the Nerve Growth Factor.

Autobiography

by Rita Levi-Montalcini

prepared for the Nobel Foundation, December 1986

My twin sister Paola and I were born in Turin on April 22, 1909, the youngest of four children. Our parents were Adamo Levi, an electrical engineer and gifted mathematician, and Adele Montalcini, a talented painter and an exquisite human being. Our older brother Gino, who died twelve years ago of a heart attack, was one of the most well known Italian architects and a professor at the University of Turin. Our sister Anna, five years older than Paola and myself, lives in Turin with her children and grandchildren. Ever since adolescence, she has been an enthusiastic admirer of the great Swedish writer, the Nobel Laureate Selma Lagerlöf, and she infected me so much with her enthusiasm that I decided to become a writer and describe an Italian saga "à la Lagerlöf." But things were to take a different turn.

The four of us enjoyed a most wonderful family atmosphere, filled with love and reciprocal devotion. Both parents were highly cultured and instilled in us their high appreciation of intellectual pursuit. It was, however, a typical Victorian style of life, all decisions being taken by the head of the family, the husband and father. He loved us dearly and had a great respect for women, but he believed that a professional career would interfere with the duties of a wife and mother. He therefore decided that the three of us—Anna, Paola and I—would not engage in studies which open the way to a professional career and that we would not enroll in the University.

Ever since childhood, Paola had shown an extraordinary artistic talent and father's decision did not prevent her full-time dedication to painting. She became one of the most outstanding women painters in Italy and is at present still in full activity. I had a more difficult time. At twenty, I realized that I could not possibly adjust to a feminine role as conceived by my father, and asked him permission to engage in a professional career. In eight months I filled my gaps in Latin, Greek and mathematics, graduated from high school, and entered medical school in Turin. Two of my university colleagues and close friends, Salvador Luria and Renato Dulbecco, were to receive the Nobel Prize in Physiology or Medicine, respectively, seventeen and eleven years before I would receive the same most prestigious award. All three of us were students of the famous Italian histologist, Giuseppe Levi. We are indebted to him for a superb training in biological science, and for having learned to approach scientific problems in a most rigorous way at a time when such an approach was still unusual.

In 1936 I graduated from medical school with a *summa cum laude* degree in Medicine and Surgery, and enrolled in the three year specialization in neurology and psychiatry, still uncertain whether I should devote myself fully to the medical profession or pursue at the same time basic research in neurology. My perplexity was not to last too long.

In 1936 Mussolini issued the "Manifesto per la Difesa della Razza," signed by ten Italian 'scientists.' The manifesto was soon followed by the promulgation of laws barring academic and professional careers to non-Aryan Italian citizens. After a short period spent in Brussels as a guest of a neurological institute, I returned to Turin on the verge of the invasion of Belgium by the German army, Spring 1940, to join my family. The two alternatives left then to us were either to emigrate to the United States, or to pursue some activity that needed neither support nor connection with the outside Aryan world where we lived. My family chose this second alternative. I then decided to build a small research unit at home and installed it in my bedroom. My inspiration was a 1934 article by Viktor Hamburger reporting on the effects of limb extirpation in chick embryos. My project had barely started when Giuseppe Levi, who had escaped from Belgium invaded by Nazis, returned to Turin and joined me, thus becoming, to my great pride, my first and only assistant.

The heavy bombing of Turin by Anglo-American air forces in 1941 made it imperative to abandon Turin and move to a country cottage where I rebuilt my mini-laboratory and resumed my experiments. In the Fall of 1943, the invasion of Italy by the German army forced us to abandon our now dangerous refuge in Piemonte and flee to Florence, where we lived underground until the end of the war.

In Florence I was in daily contact with many close, dear friends and courageous partisans of the "Partito di Azione." In August of 1944, the advancing Anglo-American armies forced the German invaders to leave Florence. At the Anglo-American Headquarters, I was hired as a medical doctor and assigned to a camp of war refugees who were brought to Florence by the hundreds from the North where the war was still raging. Epidemics of infectious diseases and of abdominal typhus spread death among the refugees, where I was in charge as nurse and medical doctor, sharing with them their suffering and the daily danger of death.

The war in Italy ended in May 1945. I returned with my family to Turin where I resumed my academic positions at the University. In the Fall of 1947, an invitation from Professor Viktor Hamburger to join him and repeat the experiments which we had performed many years earlier in the chick embryo, was to change the course of my life.

Although I had planned to remain in St. Louis for only ten to twelve months, the excellent results of our research made it imperative for me to postpone my return to Italy. In 1956 I was offered the position of Associate Professor and in 1958 that of Full Professor, a position which I held until retirement in 1977. In 1962 I established a research unit in Rome, dividing my time between this city and St. Louis. From 1969 to 1978 I also held the position of Director of the Institute of Cell Biology of the Italian National Council of Research, in Rome. Upon retirement in 1979, I became Guest Professor of this same institute.

April 22, 1909   Birth of Rita Levi-Montalcini in Turin, Italy

October 1922   King Vittorio Emmanuele II appoints Benito
Mussolini prime minister of Italy

June 10, 1924   Death of Giacomo Matteotti, beginning of rise
of Fascism in Italy

September 1930   Rita Levi-Montalcini enters Turin School of
Medicine

Timeline

April 22, 1909
Birth of Rita Levi-Montalcini
in Turin, Italy

October 16, 1938
Government proclamation that
Jewish people may not study
or work in universities or
academies of Italy

Winter 1941
Rita Levi-Montalcini turns
her bedroom into a
science laboratory and
performs experiments
on chick embryos.

1910   1920   1930   1940

September 1930
Rita Levi-Montalcini
enters Turin School
of Medicine

**September 1944
to July 1945**
Rita Levi-Montalcini works
as a medic in wartorn Italy

September 19, 1945
Rita Levi-Montalcini sails to
St. Louis, Missouri, to work
with Viktor Hamburger

November 1930 Death of Giovanna, the Levi-Montalcini's house-keeper, which inspires Rita Levi-Montalcini to dedicate her life to medicine

September 1931 Rita Levi-Montalcini begins working as a laboratory assistant for anatomist Giuseppe Levi

August 1, 1932 Death of Adamo Levi-Montalcini, Rita's father

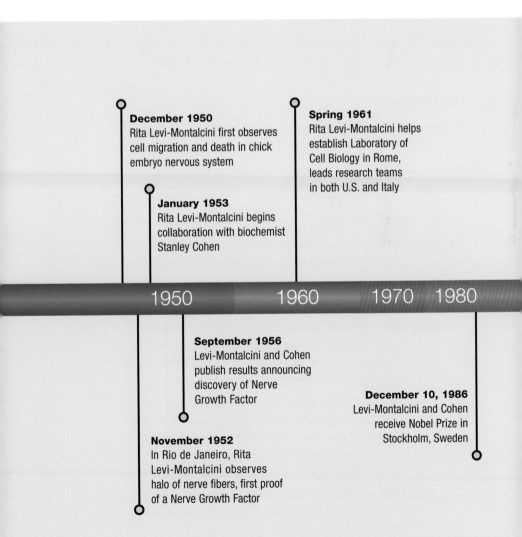

December 1950
Rita Levi-Montalcini first observes cell migration and death in chick embryo nervous system

Spring 1961
Rita Levi-Montalcini helps establish Laboratory of Cell Biology in Rome, leads research teams in both U.S. and Italy

January 1953
Rita Levi-Montalcini begins collaboration with biochemist Stanley Cohen

1950　　　　1960　　1970　1980

September 1956
Levi-Montalcini and Cohen publish results announcing discovery of Nerve Growth Factor

December 10, 1986
Levi-Montalcini and Cohen receive Nobel Prize in Stockholm, Sweden

November 1952
In Rio de Janeiro, Rita Levi-Montalcini observes halo of nerve fibers, first proof of a Nerve Growth Factor

June 1936	Rita Levi-Montalcini graduated from Turin School of Medicine *summa cum laude* in Medicine and Surgery
June 1936	Rita Levi-Montalcini enrolled in three-year specialization course of study in neurology and psychiatry, joining the Clinic for Nervous and Mental Diseases
July 14, 1938	Racist manifesto against Jews published in Italian newspapers, appearing to be signed by ten scientists
October 16, 1938	Government proclamation that Jewish people may not study or work in universities or academies of Italy
March 1939 to	
December 1939	Rita Levi-Montalcini and members of her family live in Brussels, Belgium
September 12, 1939	Germany invades Poland
May 1939	In Pact of Steel, Italy becomes war ally of Germany
June 10, 1940	Italy declares war against France and Great Britain
Summer 1940	Rita Levi-Montalcini reads and finds inspiration in Viktor Hamburger's landmark 1934 article about the nervous system in chicken embryos
Winter 1941 to	
Spring 1942	Rita Levi-Montalcini turns her bedroom into a science laboratory and performs experiments on chick embryos. In summer 1941, Giuseppe Levi joins her in her work.
Fall 1942	Allied bombing of Turin begins, and the Levi-Montalcini family moves out of the city and into the countryside. Levi-Montalcini transports her makeshift laboratory and continues experiments on chick embryos
July 1943	Italian anti-Fascists turn on Mussolini, who flees north and establishes a puppet government

September 10, 1943	German tanks arrive in Turin
October 8, 1943	Levi-Montalcinis try to flee to Switzerland but end up in hiding in Florence, Italy
September 2, 1944	British troops enter Florence, marking the beginning of the Allied liberation of Italy from Fascist and Nazi domination
September 1944 to July 1945	Rita Levi-Montalcini works as a medic in wartorn Italy
April 28, 1945	Mussolini captured and assassinated
July 1945	War over, Rita Levi-Montalcini returns to the University of Turin
September 19, 1945	Rita Levi-Montalcini sails from Genoa, Italy, destined for St. Louis, Missouri, to join the laboratory team of embryologist Viktor Hamburger
January 1950	Rita Levi-Montalcini learns of Elmer Bueker's experiments using mouse sarcoma cells to induce nerve growth in chick embryos
December 1950	Rita Levi-Montalcini observes cell migration and death in chick embryo nervous system, soon presents paper on findings at New York Academy of Sciences
September 1952	Rita Levi-Montalcini travels to Rio de Janeiro, Brazil, to work in the in vitro cell culture laboratory of Hertha Meyer
November 1952	Experiments result in remarkable halo of nerve fibers
January 1953	Rita Levi-Montalcini returns to Washington University and begins collaboration with biochemist Stanley Cohen
September 1956	Levi-Montalcini and Cohen publish results on effect of snake venom extract on nerve cell growth, announcing discovery of Nerve Growth Factor

Chronology

June 1959	Stanley Cohen leaves Washington University and joins faculty of Vanderbilt University in Nashville, Tennessee
Spring 1961	Rita Levi-Montalcini helps establish Laboratory of Cell Biology in Rome, sharing the directorship and now maintaining labs in two continents
June 1963	Death of Adele Levi-Montalcini, Rita's mother
July 1979	Rita Levi-Montalcini retires as director of Laboratory of Cell Biology in Rome, continues as researcher there
1983	California research team isolates human gene responsible for Nerve Growth Factor
October 13, 1986	The Nobel Foundation announces that its 1986 Prize for Medicine or Physiology will go jointly to Rita Levi-Montalcini and Stanley Cohen
December 10, 1986	Levi-Montalcini and Cohen receive Nobel Prize in Stockholm, Sweden
1988	Publication of *In Praise of Imperfection,* Rita Levi-Montalcini's autobiography
1993	Publication of *Il tuo futuro* (*Your Future*), Rita Levi-Montalcini's book addressing modern youth about education and values
September 28, 2000	Paola Levi-Montalcini, Rita's twin sister and living companion for years, dies
2001	Publication of *Un universo inquieto* (*An Unquiet Universe*), Rita Levi-Montalcini's book on the life and works of her sister, the artist Paola Levi-Montalcini
2002	Publication of *Tempo di mutamenti* (*Times of Change*), Rita Levi-Montalcini's book on the science of evolution and the future of humankind

Notes

Chapter 1

1. Rita Levi-Montalcini, *In Praise of Imperfection: My Life and Work*, translated by Luigi Attardi (New York: Basic Books, 1988), 83.
2. Ibid., 88.
3. Ibid., 89.
4. Ibid., 91.
5. Ibid., 92-93.
6. Viktor Hamburger, "The Effects of Wing Bud Extirpation on the Development of the Central Nervous System in Chick Embryos," *The Journal of Experimental Zoology* 68, no. 3 (1934): 490-491.
7. Rita Levi-Montalcini, "NGF: An Uncharted Route," Chapter 14 in Frederic G. Worden, Judith P. Swazey, and George Adelman, eds., *The Neurosciences: Paths of Discovery* (Cambridge, Mass., and London: MIT Press, 1975), 247.
8. Levi-Montalcini, *In Praise of Imperfection*, 93.
9. Ibid., 94.
10. Ibid., 94.
11. Ibid., 96.
12. Ibid.
13. Ibid.
14. Ibid., 96-97.
15. Ibid., 97.

Chapter 2

16. Levi-Montalcini, *In Praise of Imperfection*, 12-13.
17. "Morta Paola Levi Montalcini, sorella di Rita," 29 September 2000, *La Nazione* website, http://lanazione.quotidiano.net/art/2000/09/29/1337059. English translation by H. Wiley Hitchcock.
18. Levi-Montalcini, *In Praise of Imperfection*, 43.
19. Ibid., 75.
20. Ibid., 76.
21. Ibid., 27.
22. Ibid., 34.
23. Ibid., 35.
24. Ibid., 36.
25. Ibid., 37.
26. Ibid., 38.
27. Ibid., 41.
28. Ibid., 39.

Chapter 3

29. Levi-Montalcini, *In Praise of Imperfection*, 49.
30. Ibid., 50.
31. Ibid., 51.
32. Ibid., 55.
33. Ibid., 57.
34. Ibid., 60.
35. Ibid., 42.
36. Ibid., 45-46.
37. Ibid., 46.

Chapter 4

38. Levi-Montalcini, *In Praise of Imperfection*, 33.
39. Ibid., 34.
40. Ibid., 84.
41. Ibid., 82.
42. Ibid., 80.
43. Ibid., 84.
44. Ibid., 85.
45. Ibid., 98.
46. Ibid., 102.
47. Ibid., 105.
48. Ibid., 106.
49. Ibid., 107.

Notes

Chapter 5

50. Levi-Montalcini, *In Praise of Imperfection,* 111.

51. Ibid., 113.

52. Ibid., 113.

53. Levi-Montalcini, "NGF: An Uncharted Route," 249.

54. Levi-Montalcini, *In Praise of Imperfection,* 140-141.

55. Ibid., 141.

56. Ibid., 142.

57. Viktor Hamburger and Rita Levi-Montalcini, "Proliferation, Differentiation and Degeneration in the Spinal Ganglia of the Chick Embryo under Normal and Experimental Conditions," *The Journal of Experimental Zoology* 3 (1949): 497.

58. Levi-Montalcini, *In Praise of Imperfection,* 145.

59. Ibid., 146

60. Ibid.

61. Ibid., 147.

62. Ibid., 148.

63. Levi-Montalcini, "NGF: An Uncharted Route," 250.

64. Ibid., 251.

65. Levi-Montalcini, *In Praise of Imperfection,* 149-150.

66. Ibid., 152.

67. Levi-Montalcini, "NGF: An Uncharted Route," 252.

68. Levi-Montalcini, *In Praise of Imperfection,* 161.

69. Ibid., 162.

70. Ibid., 163.

71. Ibid.

72. Ibid.

73. Ibid.

74. Ibid., 164.

75. Levi-Montalcini, "NGF: An Uncharted Route," 253.

76. Ibid.

77. Levi-Montalcini, *In Praise of Imperfection,* 165.

78. Ibid., 166.

79. Ibid., 167.

80. Ibid., 167-168.

81. Ibid., 168.

Chapter 7

82. Levi-Montalcini, *In Praise of Imperfection,* 196.

83. Ibid.

84. Ibid., 197.

85. Rita Levi-Montalcini and Pietro Calissano, "The Nerve-Growth Factor," *Scientific American* 240, no. 6 (1979): 71.

86. Levi-Montalcini, "NGF: An Uncharted Route," 257.

87. Ibid., 261.

88. Ibid.

89. Ibid., 262.

90. Levi-Montalcini, *In Praise of Imperfection,* 189.

91. bid., 190.

92. Ibid., 202.

93. Ibid., 203.

94. Ibid., 194.

95. Ibid., 199.

96. Pietro Calissano, Antonino Cattaneo, Silvia Biocca, Luigi Aloe, Delio Mercanti, and Rita Levi-Montalcini, "The Nerve Growth Factor: Established Findings and Controversial Aspects," *Experimental Cell Research* 154 (1984): 6.

97. In Praise of Imperfection, 200.

Chapter 8

98. Levi-Montalcini, *In Praise of Imperfection,* 201.

99. Ibid.

100. Kerstin Hall, Presentation Speech, Nobel Prize for Physiology or Medicine, 1986, from the Official Web Site of The Nobel Foundation, http://www.nobel.se/medicine/laureates/1986/presentation-speech.html.

101. Ibid.

102. Ibid.

103. Ibid.

104. The Nobel Assembly at the Karolinska Institute, "The 1986 Nobel Prize in Physiology or Medicine," Press Release, October 13, 1986, from the Official Web Site of The Nobel Foundation, http://www.nobel.se/medicine/laureates/1986/press.html.

105. Ibid.

106. Rita Levi-Montalcini, "The Nerve Growth Factor 35 Years Later," *Science,* vol. 237 (9/4/87), 1154. This article was a reprint of her Nobel Prize lecture, delivered in Stockholm on December 8, 1986.

107. Ibid., 1161.

108. Jean L. Marx, "The 1986 Nobel Prize for Physiology or Medicine," *Science* 234 (1986): 544.

109. Levi-Montalcini, *In Praise of Imperfection,* 207.

110. Ibid., 209.

111. Ibid., 210-11.

112. Ibid., 105.

113. Rita Levi-Montalcini, Foreword, *A Directory of Women's Groups in Emergency Situations,* on the WIN Emergency and Solidarity web site, http://web.tiscali.it/WIN/rita.html.

114. Ibid.

115. Levi-Montalcini, *In Praise of Imperfection,* 5.

Bibliography

PRIMARY SOURCES

Calissano, Pietro, Antonino Cattaneo, Silvia Biocca, Luigi Aloe, Delio Mercanti, and Rita Levi-Montalcini. "The Nerve Growth Factor: Established Findings and Controversial Aspects." *Experimental Cell Research* 154 (1984): 1–9.

Cohen, Stanley. "Purification of a Nerve-Growth Promoting Protein from the Mouse Salivary Gland and Its Neuro-Cytotoxic Antiserum." *Proceedings of the National Academy of Sciences* 46, no. 3 (1960): 302–311.

Hamburger, Viktor. "The Effects of Wing Bud Extirpation on the Development of the Central Nervous System in Chick Embryos." *The Journal of Experimental Zoology* 68, no. 3 (1934): 449–494.

Hamburger, Viktor, and Rita Levi-Montalcini. "Proliferation, Differentiation and Degeneration in the Spinal Ganglia of the Chick Embryo under Normal and Experimental Conditions." *The Journal of Experimental Zoology* 3(1949): 457–501.

Levi-Montalcini, Rita. "From Turin to Stockholm via St. Louis and Rio de Janeiro." *Science* 287 (2000): 809.

Levi-Montalcini, Rita. *In Praise of Imperfection: My Life and Work.* Translated by Luigi Attardi. New York: Basic Books, 1988.

Levi-Montalcini, Rita. "The Nerve Growth Factor 35 Years Later." *Science* 237 (1987): 1154–1162.

Levi-Montalcini, Rita. "NGF: An Uncharted Route." Chapter 14 in Frederic G. Worden, Judith P. Swazey, and George Adelman, eds. *The Neurosciences: Paths of Discovery.* Cambridge, Mass., and London: MIT Press, 1975).

Levi-Montalcini, Rita, and Pietro U. Angeletti. "Nerve Growth Factor." *Physiological Reviews* 48, no. 3 (1968): 534–569.

Levi-Montalcini, Rita ,and Pietro Calissano. "The Nerve-Growth Factor." *Scientific American* 240, no. 6 (1979): 44–53.

Levi-Montalcini, Rita, and Stanley Cohen. "In Vitro and In Vivo Effects of a Nerve Growth-Stimulating Agent Isolated from Snake Venom." *Proceedings of the National Academy of Sciences* 42, no. 9 (1956): 695–699.

Levi-Montalcini, Rita, and Viktor Hamburger. "Selective Growth Stimulating Effects of Mouse Sarcoma on the Sensory and Sympathetic Nervous System of the Chick Embryo." *Journal of Experimental Zoology* 116, no. 2 (1951): 321–351.

SECONDARY SOURCES

Bennett, M. R., W. G. Gibson, and G. Lemon. "Neuronal Cell Death, Nerve Growth Factor and Neurotropic Models: 50 Years On." *Autonomic Neuroscience: Basic and Clinical* 95 (2002): 1–23.

Brown, Kathryn. "A Lifelong Fascination with the Chick Embryo." *Science* 290 (2000): 1284–1287.

Kirk, David L., and Garland E. Allen, III. "Viktor Hamburger: A Prepared, Persistent, and Deserving Mind Favored by Many 'Fortuities'." *Developmental Dynamics* 222 (2001): 545–551.

Marx, Jean L. "The 1986 Nobel Prize for Physiology or Medicine." *Science* 234 (1986): 543–544.

Newmark, Peter. "Growth Factors Bring Reward." *Nature* 323 (1986): 572.

Tonse N. K. Raju. "The Nobel Chronicles." *The Lancet* 355, no. 9202 (2000): 506.

WEBSITES

Stanley Cohen, Autobiography, Nobel e-Museum,
http://www.nobel.se/medicine/laureates/1986/cohen-autobio.html

Kerstin Hall, Presentation Speech, Nobel Prize for Physiology or Medicine, 1986, from the Official Web Site of The Nobel Foundation,
http://www.nobel.se/medicine/laureates/1986/presentation-speech.html

Rita Levi-Montalcini, Foreword, *A Directory of Women's Groups in Emergency Situations,* on the WIN Emergency and Solidarity web site,
http://web.tiscali.it/WIN/rita.html>

"Morta Paola Levi Montalcini, sorella di Rita," 29 September 2000, *La Nazione* website,
http://lanazione.quotidiano.net/art/2000/09/29/1337059

Bibliography

The Nobel Assembly at the Karolinska Institute, "The 1986 Nobel Prize in Physiology or Medicine," Press Release, 13 October 1986, from the Official Web Site of The Nobel Foundation, http://www.nobel.se/medicine/laureates/1986/press.html

Ronald W. Oppenheim, "Pioneer of a New Era: Viktor Hamburger and the Emergence of Experimental Embryology and Neuroembryology," *Neuroscience Newsletter* (online), http://web.sfn.org/NL/2000/May-June/articles/pioneer.html

Renato M. E. Sabbatini, *Neurons and Synapses: The History of Its Discovery,* http://www.epub.org.br/cm/n17/history/neurons1_i.htm

Women's International Network Emergency and Solidarity, *A Directory of Women's Groups in Emergency Situations,* http://web.tiscali.it/no-redirect-tiscali/WIN/index.html

Bertsch McGrayne, Sharon. *Nobel Prize Women in Science: Their Lives, Struggles, and Momentous Discoveries.* Seacaucus, N.J.: Carol Publishing Group, 1993.

Ledoux, Joseph. *Synaptic Self: How Our Brains Become Who We Are.* New York: Penguin USA, 2003.

Levi, Primo. *If This Is a Man and The Truce.* New York: Penguin Modern Classics/Viking Press, 1979.

Levi-Montalcini, Rita. *The Saga of the Nerve Growth Factor: Preliminary Studies, Discovery, Further Development* (World Scientific Series in 20th Century Biology, Vol 3). River Edge, N.J.: World Scientific Publishing Co., 1997.

Nobel e-Museum,
http://www.nobel.se/index.html

Ridley, Matt. *Genome.* New York: HarperCollins, 2000.

Watson, James D. *DNA: The Secret of Life.* New York: Knopf, 2003.

Zuccotti, Susan. *The Italians and the Holocaust: Persecution, Rescue, and Survival.* New York: Basic Books, 1997.

Index

Index

Index

page:

32: Courtesy of Rita Levi-Montalcini
33: Courtesy of Rita Levi-Montalcini
34: Courtesy of Rita Levi-Montalcini
35: Library of Congress, Prints and Photographs Division, LC-DIG-ppmsc-06635
36: © The Nobel Foundation
37: Washington University Archives, St. Louis, Missouri
38: Washington University Archives, St. Louis, Missouri
39: Washington University Archives, St. Louis, Missouri
40: © Bettmann/CORBIS
41: Courtesy of Rita Levi-Montalcini
Cover: Washington University Archives, St. Louis, Missouri

About the Author

Susan Tyler Hitchcock is the author of seven books, including *Gather Ye Wild Things: A Forager's Year; Coming About: A Family Passage at Sea;* and *The University of Virginia: A Pictorial History*. She works as an editor for the Book Division of the National Geographic Society. She wrote *Sylvia Earle* for the Chelsea House series on Women Discoverers. She holds a B.A. and M.A. in English from the University of Michigan and a Ph.D. in English from the University of Virginia. She, her husband, two children, two dogs, one cat, and four chickens make their home in the Blue Ridge Mountains near Charlottesville, Virginia.